The Theory of
Idle Resources

By the same author

THE THEORY OF COLLECTIVE BARGAINING
*London: P. S. King & Sons, 1930. New York: The Free Press,
1954. 2d Edition, London: Institute of Economic Affairs, 1975*

ECONOMISTS AND THE PUBLIC
London: Jonathan Cape, 1936

THE THEORY OF IDLE RESOURCES
London: Jonathan Cape, 1939, Indianapolis: Liberty Press, 1977

PLAN FOR RECONSTRUCTION
London: Kegan Paul, 1943

KEYNESIANISM—RETROSPECT AND PROSPECT
Chicago: Regnery, 1963. Indianapolis: Liberty Press, 1977

THE ECONOMICS OF THE COLOUR BAR
London: Institute of Economic Affairs, 1964

POLITICALLY IMPOSSIBLE . . .?
London: Institute of Economic Affairs, 1971

THE STRIKE-THREAT SYSTEM
New Rochelle, N. Y.: Arlington House, 1973

A REHABILITATION OF SAY'S LAW
Athens, Ohio: Ohio University Press, 1975

The Theory of Idle Resources

A Study in Definition
Second Edition
W. H. Hutt

Liberty*Press*

Indianapolis

Liberty Press is a publishing imprint of Liberty Fund, Inc., a foundation established to encourage study of the ideal of a society of free and responsible individuals.

The cuneiform inscription that serves as the design motif for our endpapers is the earliest known written appearance of the word "freedom" (*ama-gi*), or liberty. It is taken from a clay document written about 2300 B.C. in the Sumerian city-state of Lagash.

Library of Congress Cataloging in Publication Data
Hutt, William Harold, 1899–
    The theory of idle resources.

    Includes bibliographical references and index.
    1. Economics.   2. Keynes, John Maynard, 1883–1946. The general theory of employment, interest and money.   3. Unemployed.   I. Title.
HB199.H73   1976   330.15'6   76–26326
ISBN 0–913966–19–3

Contents

(1) Similar causes exist for idleness in labor, equipment and all other resources. (2) Idleness has one appearance but exists in several senses, (3) which require definition. (4) Popular conceptions of unemployment of labor recognized by custom and law do not help us to define "idleness." (5) The categories isolated here are based on logical rather than empirical criteria, (6) and the framers of policies ought to recognize them. (7) There can be no measure of utilization of idleness, (8) and Keynes' attempt to measure "employment" has absurd implications. (9) Pre-Keynesian theory did not, as has been alleged, assume "full employment," (10) which notion has no meaning as an absolute condition. (11) "Idling," meaning "underemployment," is a parallel conception to "idleness." (12) Criteria for definition.

(1) Valueless idle resources are those which it would not pay any individual to employ, even if no charge were made for their use. (2) The range of valuable resources may expand or contract. (3) This does not imply any

expansion or contraction in the effectiveness of the response to consumers' (or some other) sovereignty. (4) The vague phrase "increase in economic activity" can only have meaning if it refers to a fall in the proportion of valuable idle resources to all valuable resources. (5) Purely valueless equipment can have no net scrap value. (6) Resources are not valueless because the costs of depreciation cannot be earned. (7) Idle unscrapped resources possessing scrap value may be in pseudo-idleness; (8) and idle resources with capital value but no scrap or hire value are "temporarily valueless." (9) The idleness of equipment is seldom due to its being purely valueless. (10) Full utilization of existing resources is more likely to cause the range of valuable resources to expand than to contract. (11) Resources which have negative capital value but provide valuable services are unimportant. (12) Except for imbeciles, the sick and children, there are no parallels to valueless resources in labor. (13) The "unemployed" are idle for quite different reasons. (14) And natural resources which have once been valuable seldom lose all their value, so that any subsequent idleness must be due to other causes.

(1) Uncompleted equipment in process of construction must be regarded as employed; (2) and individuals add-to their powers through education, or (3) conserving their powers through rest, or (4) actively "prospecting" for remunerative jobs, may similarly be regarded as employed. (5) Pseudo-idleness is a similar but not identical condition. (6) It exists when the capital value of resources is greater than their scrap value, while their net hire value is nil. (7) The service rendered by such resources is that of "availability." (8) Pseudo-idleness can be illustrated in capital consumers' goods and capital producers' goods. (9) The "availability" may be regarded as continuously purchased in the form of capital investment until utilization takes place, or as

continuously enjoyed and consumed in the form of income; (10) and this process is taking place, even when "availability" is preserved without actual idleness. (11) The indivisibility of an efficient unit of specialized equipment is a common cause of pseudo-idleness under fluctuating or spasmodic demand, (12) and sometimes under constant demand. (13) Reserves of goods for sale, or stocks of goods in course of liquidation may be in pseudo-idleness.

(1) As skill once acquired is seldom lost, pseudo-idleness in labor due to feared loss of specialized skill is rare (2) although cases may exist. (3) But important cases arise when supplementary employments will destroy simple availability for more profitable employments. (4) Those who accordingly keep themselves attached to a trade, are paid (5) not by a retaining fee, but through favorable "expectation of earnings." (6) Similarly, if "floating labor," unattached to a particular trade, is a necessary consequence of productive technique, it is in pseudo-idleness and remunerated through "expectation of earnings." (7) The reality of such remuneration may be simply demonstrated. (8) The typical poverty of casual workers does not affect the issue. (9) The "reserves" are purchased through wage rates, and cannot be "forced" unless employers' monopoly can destroy labor mobility.

(1) Preferred idleness is found in labor only. The simplest case is preference for leisure. (2) Things like pride, prestige, boredom or laziness may lead to idleness, and being preferred to the return from employment. (3) The preference for idleness may depend upon attachment to a district where an individual has relatives or friends and a customary mode of living. (4) Given the

social will, preferred idleness implies no wrong use of resources but might be deplorable on moral grounds.
(5) Preferred idleness among the "work shy" tends to
vary according to the income available without work.
(6) There may be a preference for jobs giving intermittent leisure, (7) and if the effect is held to be "demoralizing," decasualization might be a remedy. (8) But the
"reckless" and "lazy" casual laborer may simply be
relying upon the fact that he will not be allowed to
starve.

(1) Consumers are apt to be more vigilant in respect of
the price than the quality of a commodity. (2) Similarly,
workers in general tend to be more concerned about
wage rates than about the purchasing power of wages,
and in depressions may collectively prefer unemployment to employment at lower wage rates. (3) Keynes
seems to argue that much idleness is due to this cause
which, he implies, orthodox economists overlooked.
(4) But although the conception of "irrational preferences" lies outside the province of "pure theory,"
except as data, this has not meant blindness to their
existence; (5) for the orthodox have realistically recognized the significance of such preferences in relation to
scarcity through the conception of "net advantageousness." (6) It is the statesman rather than the economist
who is concerned with the avoidance of the results of
irrationality in preferences. (7) But in any case, *other*
sources of irrationality are probably much more serious.

(1) Resources are in participating idleness when their
idle existence confers the right to participate in monopoly revenues. (2) The condition may arise under a

restrictive quota scheme. (3) But resources may actually attach themselves in idleness to a monopolized trade because of participation rights obtainable. (4) Unless complete mergers are possible, unused capacity is likely to be maintained for "quota hunting" (5) although, since participating idleness militates against harmonious output restriction, other distributive arrangements may be sought. (6) Interloping resources may be attracted in *to share in the chance* of employment in a monopolized field. The consequent participating idleness may be illustrated by the example of petrol retailing. (7) "Participating idleness" may easily be confused with "pseudo-idleness" or "aggressive idleness."

(1) Participating idleness in labor is most clear under "short-time" work with "work-sharing" motives, the monopoly revenues being shared equally, (2) and cessation of recruitment being a means of sharing them among a declining number. (3) Participating rights are not conferred on a worker accepting another employment. (4) An excluded worker may remain unemployed and attached to a monopolized trade because his availability increases his *chance* of the privileged employment it may offer; (5) and even if temporary employment would not destroy his availability it might weaken his *right* to privileged employment. (6) Interlopers may be *attracted in* to share in the *chance* of employment in a monopolized field. The consequent participating idleness may be illustrated by the example of stockbrokers, (7) or the medical profession, (8) or certain poorly paid casual trades; (9) in the latter cases, the odium attaching to the employers of low-paid labor having the same consequence as wage fixation (10) and acting as an important contributory cause of the casual nature of such employments. In these circumstances, decasualization is inequitable. (11) Work-sharing ar-

rangements resemble the quota systems of cartels, and unemployment benefits paid out of union funds resemble cartel bonuses to compensate for the withdrawal of output. (12) But, unlike unemployment benefits, cartel bonuses are not contingent upon the continued idleness of the resources in alternative employments. (13) In practice, State-subsidized unemployment benefits support general restrictionism in the labor market and are contingent upon absolute idleness. (14) But cartel arrangements are voluntary in a sense in which labor restrictions are not. (15) For justice, the compensation conferred by a union's unemployment pay should be complete; (16) and this would be insisted upon if the members of a trade union regarded it as shareholders do a firm. (17) But organized labor has usually been hostile to the dilution of monopoly revenues through work sharing. (18) The failure of the poor to share their poverty is the most neglected aspect of the unemployment problem.

(1) Resources excluded from or withheld from monopolized employments must, if they remain idle, be idle in some other sense also. (2) "Enforced idleness" is caused by the exclusion of resources during the monopolization of production; but the term has a limited meaning (3) and must be distinguished from two other forms of "waste": (i) specialized "diverted resources" which happen to find inferior employments, and (ii) the hypothetical resources which might have become specialized in the monopolized field but for powers of exclusion. (4) "Diverted labor resources" may be described as in "disguised unemployment," but the condition is unimportant in relation to other forms of waste which are not expressed in idleness. (5) "Enforced idleness" may be caused by the monopolization of cooperant stages of production.

large public utilities, natural monopoly is of relatively small importance.

(1) The distribution of monopoly gains among cooperant monopolists is indeterminate, and may depend upon "reasonableness" or (2) bargaining, in which case "strike idleness" may arise. (3) When competing firms operate over more than one set of cooperant productive processes, distribution may be arranged through "demarcations," which may be enforced by strikes. (4) "Strike idleness" does not arise from "withheld capacity" unless a cooperant producer resists in order to force a sharing of the monopoly gains. (5) "Aggressive idleness" arises from the maintenance of unutilized capacity with a view to aggressive selling against potential interlopers.

(1) This essay has concentrated on "idleness" issues, and ignored "demand" issues. (2) But our analysis of idleness has introduced distinctions which are essential for any satisfactory study of the effects of demand variations. (3) The application of our conceptions to monetary theory has yet to be done (4) although the conceptions are directly serviceable in studies of the non-monetary aspects of idleness and (5) the trade cycle, and (6) may suggest the correct approach to the monetary aspects of idleness. (7) Wasteful idleness arises through the restriction of competition.

(1) "Money," as we have defined it, (2) is never subject to the forms of idleness we have distinguished for non-money, (3) but it is as productive as all assets, (4) even when held speculatively. (5) What has been termed

"idle money" is really in "pseudo-idleness." (6) Money does not render its services by circulating but by being held ready to circulate. (7) A money unit conforms to ordinary laws of value. (8) The determinants of the nominal money supply (9) must be distinguished from the determinants of the aggregate real value of money. (10) As with other assets, money may be wastefully used. (11) Banking institutions may exploit, (12) but unproductive investment in money is essentially wasteful use, not idleness.

Preface to the
Second Edition

Thirty-eight years ago—half my life ago, just before the outbreak of World War II—I was goaded into writing this book, chiefly because of my intense dissatisfaction with the notion of "unemployment" of labor in Keynes' *General Theory of Employment, Interest, and Money* (1936). But I had been irritated for several years at the loose manner in which I felt economists had handled this question.

I claimed, in 1939, that I was not presenting a fundamentally original thesis, but a clarification of what I thought was "pure orthodoxy" of the pre-Keynesian kind. I was merely trying to express, with greater conceptual rigor, what had been generally understood and accepted by economists in what Keynes had called the "classical" tradition. I welcome the opportunity of now bringing out a second edition because, although the first edition had shortcomings of exposition and content which are now obvious to me, I believe that this was mainly because of its having been a pioneer effort dealing with an important but neglected issue.

Unfortunately the work did not receive from reviewers the unfavorable criticism it deserved. I recall only two exceptions. Sir Arnold Plant provided useful, candid criti-

cism in *Economica.*[1] Saying that the book "ought to be
widely read," he warned that my "exposition is not invari-
ably satisfying," although "readers will surely recognize the
importance of many of the distinctions, which are drawn
"for the most part with an admirable combination of clarity
and subtlety." Professor Lindley Fraser, in the *Economic
Journal,*[2] denied three claims on the dust cover: (1) that
the book was "largely devoted to criticism of Mr. Keynes'
General Theory," (2) that the book had shown "there must
be complete freedom of competition to allow the price
system to register consumers' wants," and (3) that it developed "the theme of what type of institutions are required by
a competitive system." These denials will be referred to in
new text to be added in the form of notes to and comments
on the original text, in chapter appendices. The reader will
then be able to consider whether or not the claims in the
cover blurb of 1939 were justified. Professor Fraser's review
was by no means hostile. He said that much of the argument
was "interesting and illuminating," but that what it *actually*
did was "to classify and examine types (or senses) of 'idleness' and to provide . . . readers with an impressive array of
new terms for the various kinds of idleness distinguished."
This effort he described as "short, stimulating and somewhat
unsatisfactory."

The words "somewhat unsatisfactory" were somewhat
lenient! But the criticism did not refer to the specific defects
that I myself now perceive. The publisher's blurb could
certainly have claimed, however, that the book was an
attempt to expose a serious weakness in a fundamental

---

[1] A. PLANT, *Economica,* May 1940.

[2] L. M. FRASER, *Economic Journal,* December 1939.

notion in the *General Theory,* namely "unemployment," either as a measurable phenomenon or as a rigorously defined condition.

Accordingly, I now provide my own criticisms of the 1939 text (1) in notes and comments which form appendices to each of the original chapters, (2) in a new Introduction, and (3) in an Addendum on "The Concept of Idle Money." Otherwise the text is reprinted just as it had then appeared, with all its weaknesses. Except for the correction of a wrong page reference and a wrong date, the incorporation of what had originally been appendices into the text of two chapters, the adoption of American spelling, consistency of style and renumbered footnotes, no change has been made in the text. The temptation to substitute American *words* for English *words* has, however, been resisted in order to emphasize that, apart from the additional text mentioned above, the book was written in South Africa before World War II, so that any topicality is accidental. For instance, the word "petrol" for "gasoline" has been retained.

The 1939 text explicitly excluded from discussion what many economists (both before and following the *General Theory*) considered to be the important "problem" of idle money. Widespread idleness of nonmoney was regarded as due, in part, to money not doing its job, not being used enough, not circulating sufficiently rapidly, not being spent quickly enough. As recession or depression emerged, it all seemed to be due to a general failure to buy everything produced, and it was felt that what pre-Keynesian economists sometimes called "money hoarding" or "idle money" had to share the blame. My first draft of the first edition dealt briefly with this issue, as well as the concept of "aggregate demand," but on the advice of F. A. Hayek, I think, I eventually omitted that part of the discussion in the published version. I was warned that in the climate of academic opinion at the time, to point too specifically to the implications would inhibit consideration of my analysis. Accordingly, I stated: "I have been wisely advised not to touch on any of the major controversies" raised by the *General Theory* three years earlier. Actually, in Chapter XII of the original edition, the relevance of "idleness issues" to "demand issues" *is* considered. But I now judge that it would be unfruitful to explore the problem further. This I do in the Addendum on "The Concept of Idle Money" and in some of the chapter appendices incorporated into this edition.

In the chapter appendices there are far more references to my own past contributions than to the works of other economists.[3] That is not because I do not feel that I am indebted to others. Indeed, I still think that I am doing nothing more than explaining what economists generally would have been teaching today had they not been lost for so long in the Keynesian jungle.

The model of the economic system I have constructed has been subject to my own continuous criticism through my attempts at reconciliation of my convictions with the conclusions of others. My notes and comments in the

---

[3] For this reason I use abbreviations in appendix footnotes for all references to such books of mine as I frequently quote, apart from the first mention, in accordance with the following schedule:

Full Title	*Abbreviation*
Keynesianism—Retrospect and Prospect	*Keynesianism*
The Theory of Collective Bargaining, 2d ed.	*Collective Bargaining,* 2d ed.
A Rehabilitation of Say's Law	*Say's Law*
The Strike-Threat System	*Strike-Threat*

chapter appendices indicate how far my understanding has benefited since 1939 from this process. But the mere fact that I have thought it best to leave the original text unchanged surely suggests either the basic soundness of the pre-Keynesian "orthodoxy" I thought I was explaining, or a personal quality which the reader may interpret as steadfastness or obdurateness.

Since the first edition, what I judge to have been the most useful contributions to an understanding of the problems of idle resources have been recent: an impressive empirical study by Professor Martin Feldstein, entitled "The Economics of the New Unemployment,"[4] and treatments of unemployment in two fine textbooks—*University Economics,* by Alchian and Allen,[5] and *Toward Economic Understanding,* by Heyne and Johnson.[6] Where Alchian and Allen's work makes its most distinctive contribution, in this and other contexts, is in the high emphasis its authors place on the productiveness of information-gathering in the economy as a whole. This leads them to perceive, when they treat the question of idleness in labor, that, in the words I used in 1939, "individuals actively 'prospecting' for remunerative jobs are employed." As Alchian and Allen put it, so-called "unemployed" persons who are genuinely looking for other jobs are "information seeking," and as such they are productively employed.[7]

Where I differ from these economists is in respect of their

---

[4] *The Public Interest,* Fall 1973.

[5] A. A. ALCHIAN and W. R. ALLEN, *University Economics,* Third Edition, Wadsworth Publishing Co., Belmont, Ca., 1972.

[6] PAUL HEYNE and THOMAS JOHNSON, *Toward Economic Understanding,* Science Research Associates, Palo Alto, Ca., 1976. Heyne and Johnson acknowledge their indebtedness to Feldstein and Alchian and Allen.

[7] ALCHIAN and ALLEN, *op. cit.,* p. 516.

perseverance with the notion that wasteful "unemployment" of labor is in some way a consequence of insufficient aggregate demand. For instance, although Feldstein recognizes that "any possible increase in aggregate demand that does not have unacceptable effects on the rate of inflation would leave a high residue of unemployment," he still feels that "management of aggregate demand has a role to play,"[8] even if its role is a minor one. I continue to insist, however, that the *only* tendency that unanticipated inflation has to mitigate wasteful idleness in men and assets is due to its crude coordinative consequences upon relative prices. The improved coordination (which could have been more efficiently and less unjustly achieved without inflation, if politics had not prevented it)[9] causes investment in larger inputs to be prospectively profitable, each such instance tending to set into operation the dynamic consequences of Say's law.

I differ from Heyne and Johnson on the same point. Their really excellent treatment of labor "unemployment" phenomena, to which I shall later refer, fails to explain the inanity of all theories which do not build on the perception that truly involuntary idleness of men (usually with concomitant idleness in assets) is *always due and solely due* to a defect in the administration of the pricing mechanism. It is when market-clearing prices (for inputs or outputs) are exceeded that men or assets are diverted into sub-optimal employments or into idleness (in one or more of the senses I

---

[8] This concession to Keynesian orthodoxy may be due, I am inclined to think, to defensive polemics on Feldstein's part—a strategy for getting a hearing.

[9] See HUTT, *Politically Impossible . . . ?,* Institute of Economic Affairs, London, 1971, pp. 28–31.

distinguish). Then it is that aggregate production, or aggregate output, or aggregate supply, or aggregate income (or whatever else we like to call it), which is the source of all demands out of income, falls short of its attainable magnitude. And when government toleration of collusive resistance to price adjustments called for by changes in (a) consumer preferences, (b) entrepreneurial judgments, (c) the innovation process and (d) the economizing process, in response to the social discipline of the market, or when inflexible prices due to mere inertia hinder the coordination of the economy in a similar manner, a prospective contraction in the flow of income causes certain wage-rates and prices which had formerly been near or at market-clearing levels to begin to exceed or diverge further from those levels. In that manner, a cumulative withholding of productive capacity is brought about. Such are, I maintain, the basic causes of depression, of the aggravation of sub-optimal use of assets and men, as well as of their wasteful idleness. The fact that unanticipated inflation *may mitigate* the wasteful chain reaction so caused, and that deflation *may worsen it,* does not enable us to blame the working of the monetary system or insufficient aggregate demand.

Note

An asterisk in the margin of a paragraph in the main text indicates that it is criticized or supplemented in a note or comment in the appendix to the chapter. A number in the margin of an appendix indicates the paragraph in the main text that is criticized or supplemented.

W. H. Hutt

University of Dallas
1976

It is curious that so important a subject as unemployment should have brought forth no treatise devoted to theoretical analysis of the condition. There have been many books purporting to deal with unemployment of labor, but these have either been descriptive works, like Sir William Beveridge's famous *Unemployment, a Problem of Industry,* or theoretical studies of demand, like Professor Pigou's *Theory of Unemployment,* or Mr. J. M. Keynes' *General Theory of Employment, Interest, and Money.* This essay tries to fill the gap. The necessity became clear to me in the course of an attempt to envisage the institutions required for an equalitarian or competitive society. Having found no satisfactory analysis of conceptions which it seemed essential to employ, I was forced to provide my own textbook treatment.

My reason for using the term "idleness" instead of "unemployment" is that the latter term has, by tradition, become associated with the idleness of labor, and any satisfactory study must obviously be concerned with "idleness" in *all* resources. And having made "idleness" my topic, I have adhered strictly to it, and do not claim to have made any direct contribution to monetary or trade-cycle theory. I was at first tempted to venture into this province, but after many wanderings I could not feel satisfied that I had found my bearings with sufficient accuracy to try to guide others. Nevertheless, I have indicated a region which ought to be explored with the instruments that I have provided. My several critical references to the work of Mr. J. M. Keynes are due to the fact that his *General Theory* happens to be in the thoughts of all economists today. I have been wisely advised not to touch on any of the major controversies which his contribution has aroused. Certainly I have not avoided controversial topics. But it is my hope that all sides in the current debate on the monetary causes of idleness will find my analysis realistic and useful, and that it will be of some help to them in searching for the origin of their differences.

Although I am offering a "theoretical" contribution, a mere contribution to conceptual clarity, my inspiration has throughout been the closest interest in practical affairs. The objective problem of inventing institutions which could foster security and equality has been the motive which has guided my study at each stage. I earnestly believe that policymakers could find enlightenment in it. But I am sufficient of a realist to know that the chances of its exercising any influence on policy are small. The politicians in unemployment-cursed countries are too concerned with their immediate popularity to give much consideration to a dispassionate analysis such as I have attempted. For if they do glance at its pages they will soon see that its implications cannot be easily reconciled with ideologies to which they feel they must of necessity pander.

However, to encourage the policymakers, I have endeavored to treat the subject, as far as possible, in a nontechnical way. Any patient and intelligent layman should be able to understand my argument. I have reduced the current jargon and conventional technical conceptions to a minimum, and where I have employed them, their meaning should be sufficiently evident to the careful reader. In this way, my treatment differs from all the recent theoretical studies of demand which intend to deal with the causes of idleness. My suggestions need not be taken on authority. The reader who is unacquainted with the economic textbooks may follow my reasoning from point to point and himself decide on its validity. I welcome the layman not, as Mr. Keynes does in his *General Theory,* as an "eavesdropper," but as one who can and should consider my thesis. I do not claim, however, to have produced a "popular" work. Where I have thought it helpful, I have not shrunk from exploiting the most abstract conceptions. And I have incidentally introduced a new jargon of my own. Hence, the reader who is inexpert in economics must persevere and have constant recourse to the summaries which may guide him through a labyrinth of notions.

It has not been my task in this essay to recommend specific reforms. Certainly I have hinted at desirable changes, but my aim here has been to determine causes. If would-be reformers feel bewildered by the practical difficulties which my analysis of causes discloses, they may be helped by my own attempt to face the basic obstacles in my *Economists and the Public,* chapter XXI, entitled "Vested Interests and the Distributive Scheme." The clue to the understanding of the chief economic and sociological problems of today can be found, in my opinion, in a recognition of the struggle which is in progress against the disrupting equalitarian effects of competitive capitalism. Competition and capitalism are hated today because of their tendency to destroy poverty and privilege more rapidly than custom and the expectations established by protections can allow. We accordingly find private interests combining to curb this process and calling upon the State to step in to do the same; and unless the resistance is expressed through monetary policy, the curbing takes the form of restrictions on production. Hence there arises a clash between what I have called the "productive scheme" and the "distributive scheme"; and wasteful idleness, both in labor and in physical things, appears to be due to the consequent restraint of productive power—a restraint imposed immediately in defense of private interests, but ultimately appearing to be reasonable and just because it defends an existing and customary distribution.

The original typescript of this book was completed more than two years before the present version was sent to the publishers. Several copies were put into circulation and I received advice and encouragement from so many friends that it is impossible to make adequate acknowledgments. But I have a special debt of gratitude to the following who at different times read the whole of the typescript as it then stood and whose comments led to substantial changes of terminology, exposition or content: Professor Lionel Robbins, Mr. Frank Paish, Professor Arnold Plant, Professor F. A. Hayek and Mr. H. A. Shannon.

W. H. Hutt

University of Cape Town
1939

The Theory of
Idle Resources

Introduction

In the new perspective which another 38 years of study of the topic of this book has revealed, it can now be usefully suggested that any inquiry into the nature and causes of idleness in resources must be concerned primarily with *one of three possible manifestations of a disease* to which a "free" or "nontotalitarian" economy is susceptible. *The disease is discoordination of the economic system* caused through defects in the administration of the pricing mechanism.[1] The word "free" refers to an economy in which loss-avoidance, profit-seeking entrepreneurial incentives are confronted with *democratic* consumers' sovereignty.[2]

The origin of the disease in its most virulent forms may be diagnosed as due to collusive or governmental overruling of the market-clearing values which the process of competition establishes.[3] The *manifestations* of the disease are

---

[1] See W. H. HUTT, *Keynesianism—Retrospect and Prospect,* Regnery, Chicago, 1963, Chap. IV, "The Nature of Coordination Through the Price System."

[2] For a definition of *"democratic* consumers' sovereignty," see footnote 5, p. 219.

[3] For an explanatory definition of the process of "competition," see p. 154.

initially and conspicuously either (1) unanticipated inflation *or* (2) unemployment of men and assets, and *ultimately
and inconspicuously,* (3) sub-optimal employment of men
and assets. Whenever the prices of inputs or outputs are
forced above, or for other reasons have been *left above*
what had previously been their market-clearing values,
then on the assumption that it is politically impossible to
eradicate those private restraints (imposed by government
or collusion) which prevent market-clearing adjustments,
one conspicuous manifestation of the disease—inflation—
seems to be avoidable only through the appearance of the
other conspicuous manifestation—wasteful idleness. But
when inflation becomes anticipated, both manifestations are
likely to exist concurrently. We then have inflation, not
deflation, being blamed for unemployment. "Stagflation,"
as the condition has been recently termed, will endure either
until the discoordination is cured, or until it is hidden in
the third, *inconspicuous* form of the disease, namely, "sub-
optimal employment," or what we termed in 1939 (after
Mrs. Joan Robinson) "disguised unemployment" or "diverted capacity."

The term "sub-optimal employment" is a much more
appropriate term for the condition, and in the critical and
explanatory notes and comments in the chapter appendices,
we use this term. Superficially, manifestation of the disease
in "sub-optimal employment" seems to be the least harmful
form. In reality, we are about to suggest, it is a symptom of
the most malignant consequence of impoverishing discoordination.

We can now usefully repeat that all three consequences
of discoordination we have noticed are caused through the
fixing of prices (including the price of labor), or the deter-

mination of input and output magnitudes, not through the pressure of *social forces* observable as the perpetual substitutions of preferred commodities or lower-cost methods of production and marketing, but through the expression of *private forces*. By "private forces" we mean price or output determinations in the interests of those workers or investors[4] who are allowed to act collusively, or who wield private coercive power *in other ways* (e.g., through government), in order to engross the most remunerative opportunities for themselves. This they can do when they are allowed to shut in or shut out men or assets from the most productive activities.

The above italicized phrase "in other ways" envisages a different channel of expression for "private forces," including the fixing of prices, or input and output magnitudes, by government, in the private interests of "pressure groups." Corporations or unions may reward legislators (by control of votes or pecuniary contributions) for laws or administrative decisions which override the social discipline of the market.[5] But the same results *may* occur through the belief that some ethical or aesthetic end which people as individuals ought to demand but do not demand, or somehow cannot individually seek, is thereby achievable. If such a belief is valid, the objective sought (an ecological benefit, for instance) must be regarded as a product, the cost of which is the sacrifice of other kinds of human well-being.

---

[4] The word "investors" refers *inter alia* to stockholders.

[5] "The true . . . explanation of extensive unemployment . . . is caused by a distortion of the system of *relative* prices and wages. And it can be corrected only by . . . the establishment in each section of the economy of those prices and wages at which supply will equal demand." F. A. HAYEK, *Full Employment at Any Price,* Institute of Economic Affairs, London, 1975, p. 19.

We have shown elsewhere[6] that, of the two forms in which symptoms of the disease are *conspicuous,* inflation is by far the more insidious. Like cancer, in its early stages it is much less painful than unemployment and loses fewer votes.

But we propose to argue further that the third, relatively *inconspicuous* and *ultimate* manifestation of the disease, namely, the employment of men and assets in sub-optimal activities, is even more detrimental to society; for it mitigates the pains of inflation as well as reduces the conspicuous idleness of human and physical resources. It concerns men and assets *forced out* of or *excluded from* the more productive kinds of employment but absorbed into less remunerative activities. Through private overruling of the market process the aggregate assets stock of a country assumes a less productive structure, adapted to the less valuable complementary skills of people laid off from, or prevented from entering, the better remunerated employment outlets.

Entrepreneurs searching for and discovering prospectively profitable production opportunities for workers shut out from more productive jobs through the power of organized labor are often denounced. They are described as "sweaters" who "take advantage of" the absence of better paid employment outlets. The labor inputs in which the entrepreneurs invest are "sweated labor." But such entrepreneurs are innocent; on the contrary, they ameliorate injustices.[7] Their thrift and risk-taking mitigate the burden on those who would otherwise have been forced to accept

---

[6] HUTT, *Keynesianism,* pp. 43–44, 173–79.

[7] In the main text this question is discussed in Chap. VIII, pp. 162–65.

work of even lower remuneration (unless such workers happened to prefer idleness).[8]

Nevertheless, owing to society and the victims themselves being unable to diagnose the causes of their low productive powers, the situation perpetuates itself. Entrepreneurs are universally vigilant in seeking out and using idle resources in men and assets. Hence there never appears to be any urgency about the wastes and injustices of workers confined to relative poverty. Think of how easily about 800,000 *illegal* immigrants who enter the United States annually get jobs.[9]

We must not leave the impression, however, that it is only people in the lower income groups who may be in suboptimal employments (together with the assets which are their tools). The condition spreads right through the economic system wherever private or governmental efforts are made to redistribute income via the nonmarket determination of inputs, outputs or prices.

It is important to warn at the outset that there are false symptoms of the various idleness phenomena. We find *apparent* idleness which in fact is either a productive state or an economic end achieved. (For instance, leisure or the "idleness" of park land from which agriculture, industry or housing are excluded, may simply be a reference to the expression of a private or collective preference.) This is treated in chapters III and IV.

The reader should bear in mind throughout that this book first appeared after a long period of serious unemployment of labor in Britain and was influenced thereby. The

[9] See p. 119.
[8] See Chap. V.

unemployment burden had been alleviated somewhat after the British devaluation of 1931, in spite of the era of competitive world inflation then initiated. But already, in 1939, it was obvious to us that the disease was gradually and insidiously assuming what we have argued is the more harmful form, namely, inflation. Moreover, the unseen burden of diverted capacity—what we now call "sub-optimal employment"—appeared to have been growing.

During the war years, however, the problems on which this essay seeks to throw the light of conceptual clarity ceased to be a matter of great public concern. And after the war governments almost universally found themselves using inflation to reduce the real values of wage-rates and prices (unjustly including those not coercively fixed) in order to avoid too much unemployment of labor. The extermination of potential demands for products in general, through the pricing of a wide range of inputs and outputs above market-clearing values, especially in unionized sectors of the economy, had become chronic; strikes and the fear of strikes were persistently threatening recession; the "new economists" interpreted the situation as due to a lagging "aggregate demand" or a deficiency of "effective demand"; and they proclaimed that recession could be rectified by an expansion of aggregate money-spending power (as distinct from aggregate purchasing power) via the fiscal form of monetary policy. "Aggregate demand" was "ineffective," they said, through an insufficient quantity of money or an unduly slow spending of it. But unless "aggregate effective demand" means "demands in general" in the Say's law sense of "supplies in general," these concepts are spurious and divert attention from the depressing effects of *underproduction* caused by pricing inputs and out-puts beyond the reach of uninflated income. We hope to show in the new Addendum on "The Concept of Idle Money" that the condition we call "pseudo-idleness" is the only idleness condition (among those we have identified) that can exist in money assets, and that actually it is a productive condition.

If we understand the significance of Say's law of markets and accept Say's definitions of "production" (as "the crea-tion of value") and "consumption" (as "the extermination of value"), we perceive that "effective demand" in any acceptable connotation is simply that part of the flow of productive services which is priced for market clearance.[10] This flow, which is incapable of being meaningfully repre-sented in demand curve form, is either (1) consumed as the services are rendered, or (2) incorporated into a stock of as-sets of varying prospective economic life-spans. Part (2) either replaces, fully or partly, the value being concurrently consumed (of services or of assets exterminated), or con-tributes to the net accumulation of assets. If the concept of "effective" has any meaning at all in this context, it must be intended to distinguish the *potential* aggregate "creation of value" from which demands (i.e., supplies) are ex-pressed, and the *actual* (i.e., "effective") aggregate creation of value, namely, those parts of the potential source of supplies which, being priced for market clearance, are expressed as demands for whatever noncompeting assets or services they are destined to be exchanged for (including

---

[10] That part which is not so priced is *wastefully* consumed (i.e., its value is exterminated), instead of being embodied in the assets stock.

money assets and monetary services among the assets stock and the services flow).[11] But types of wasteful "idleness" (as distinct from productive "idleness") originate in the failure of the social framework to create or protect incentives to price inputs and outputs at market-clearing values. Our main concern in this book is, however, not only with how wasteful idleness originates. Of greater interest is why it endures, why resources withheld or excluded from one use are not devoted to producing something else (in a sub-optimal field, of course).

Money is relevant to "effective demand" only because *unanticipated* inflation can, in a very crude way, cause certain prices which have been forced above market-clearing levels (causing therefore nonuse or underuse of men and assets) to become market-clearing values, thereby releasing "withheld" potential productive capacity and increasing "effective demand" in our sense *and* in Keynes' sense. In the original text we remind the reader several times, and especially in chapter XII, that we were wisely advised to refrain from dealing with this issue, although we are in fact forced at times to refer to it. But as we explain in our new Preface (pp. 17–18), we believe now that the omission obscures the relevance of our argument to policy. Our discussions in the last few pages of this Introduction, and in comments in the chapter appendices, are intended briefly to fill the gap. We have, however, dealt with the issues several times in other contributions.[12]

In Britain of the 1930s, in the absence of an inflationary

---

[11] See W. H. HUTT, *A Rehabilitation of Say's Law,* Ohio University Press, Athens, 1975, pp. 24 *et seq.*

[12] *The Theory of Collective Bargaining,* 2d ed., Institute of Economic Affairs, London, 1975; *Keynesianism; Say's Law.*

policy, a cumulative contraction of the wages and income flow would have forced legislation to curb the wages-reducing and profits-reducing practices of the unions and other monopolies, mostly government created. Otherwise a growing proportion of nonversatile productive capacity would have been left unutilizable. Nevertheless, during the post-World War II period, in spite of creeping, crawling, chronic inflation, unemployment of labor was never eradicated. Inflationary measures merely kept it in check. The method seemed tolerable enough as long as the majority of consumers and producers could be relied upon not to perceive what was happening.

But now, in the 1970s, we have both manifestations of the disease accompanying one another. Unanticipated inflation has increasingly become anticipated inflation; and this means, as we have remarked above and as we have been trying to show for many years,[13] that "full employment," sought by fiscal or other monetary means, comes slowly to require *accelerating inflation*. When inflation is generally expected, it becomes purposeless. Governments find it increasingly difficult to mislead the community about the planned speed of rising prices, or about the duration of those lulls in the process which appear to be technically essential for the public's continuous deception. Costs begin to be pushed up ahead of price increases; there may be a growing insistence upon "escalator clauses"; the nominal market rate of interest rises formidably to compensate for the predicted fall in real value of the money unit; gilt-edged securities begin to offer higher yields than common stocks; and *unemployment has to be accepted almost as a normal*

---

[13] For a discussion of the purposelessness of anticipated inflation, see *Keynesianism*, pp. 127–30.

accompaniment of inflation, even of accelerating inflation.[14]

In the circumstances which have been created, the achievement of an efficient, coordinated economic system requires, we suggest, the rescue of market relationships from the sectionalist restraints we have indicated. The alternatives are (a) resignation to wasteful idleness, or (b) the wasteful diversion of resources into sub-optimal production.

Interpretations of today's observed situation are not easy. The interactions of inflation, income transfers (with the consequential squandering of wage-multiplying capital),[15] exacerbation of the resulting disorder by wage and price controls, strike-threat pressures culminating in "wage-push," population growth and immigration, and—the main *countervailing* force—technological progress, have hindered empirical discernment of the determinants of wasteful idleness. Increasing taxation (overt or hidden) has been another complicating factor. It has certainly redistributed income, *perhaps temporarily for the benefit of the relatively poor.*[16] But this has been achieved at the expense of (1) restraints on the growth of the people's assets stock in response

---

[14] "The least understood" consequence of inflation "is that in the long run it inevitably produces extensive unemployment." F. A. HAYEK, *Full Employment at Any Price,* p. 49.

[15] As a leading British Socialist, Evan Durbin, regarded it (in 1940). E. M. F. DURBIN, *The Politics of Democratic Socialism,* Augustus M. Kelley, Clifton, N.J.

[16] As we have shown elsewhere (*Collective Bargaining,* 2d ed., pp. 88–93), under the welfare state we in fact find income transfers from the politically weak to the politically strong, from the thrifty to the thriftless, from the industrious to the indolent, from the responsible to the irresponsible, from the enterprising to the unenterprising, from the relatively productive to the relatively unproductive, from the successful to the unsuccessful as well as from the lucky to the unlucky. The *incentive* issue so raised is not, however, among the issues to be discussed here.

to their desire to provide for the future; (2) adverse effects upon the wage-multiplying power of assets; (3) a piling up of the national debt, "the people's collectively owned negative capital," with a mounting burden on posterity; and (4) destruction of the incentives for every individual to maximize his (and his assets') contribution to society's real income.

On the positive side, technological progress, a rapid growth of potential productive power due to scientific, capital- and labor-economizing advances, especially automation and computerization, and the development of labor-economizing managerial techniques have so far made this impoverishment process *bearable* by raising the real value of employment outlets as a whole. But the very fruitfulness of economizing innovations seems to have permitted grave defects in the coordinative mechanism to remain undiagnosed. And as we have just seen, the availability of "suboptimal employments" has obscured rather than exposed the depressive consequences. For the conspicuous wasteful idleness or idling of men and assets is a *temporary* phenomenon. The waste tends to be *permanent*.

Our reference in the previous paragraph to labor-economizing developments "raising the real value of employment outlets" may cause some readers to think that the word "raising" is a misprint for "reducing"! It is not. In the United States we are constantly hearing demands for governments to "create employment" via the squandering of resources on various kinds of boondoggling projects. But to cause more "jobs" to be available at any given remuneration, or to cause an unchanged number of "jobs" to be available at higher remuneration, can be achieved only through *the elimination of barriers* which (1) hinder the setting of market-clearing values for inputs and outputs, or (2) weaken incentives for the achievement of labor-economizing as well as capital-economizing innovations. As we have explained elsewhere,

> The improving real income of the wage-earning and salaried classes has been the consequence of (a) . . . the "economizing displacement" process, namely, managerial, technological and scientific ingenuities which have progressively displaced labor and assets from their existing employments, *thereby releasing effort and resources for providing additional—usually different—outputs,* and (b) thrift—the net *accumulation of output-yielding assets—resources which magnify the real yield to human effort.*
> Society has learned how to replace and accumulate assets in an increasingly efficient form, and how to use the services of people in an increasingly efficient manner. The phrase "increasingly efficient" refers to (i) the *composition of* replacement and accumulation of assets, and (ii) the organization of labor, *both occurring increasingly in economizing-displacement forms.* The achievement of given outputs with fewer workers, and with assets of reduced real value, is continuously rendering workers redundant in their existing occupations and specializations, and rendering assets obsolescent or obsolete in their existing form. The process is the most progressive dynamic force in economic activity because, in releasing a proportion of people and assets from their existing occupations, it leaves them available for the production of additional real income. In the absence of governmental or private restraints on the utilization of the displaced productive power, it adds to the source of demands in general and, in turn, *raises the real values at which employment outlets can be profitably offered.*[17]

If the significance of what we have called "the economizing-displacement process" is understood, the whole question

---

[17] W. H. HUTT, *The Strike-Threat System,* Arlington House, New Rochelle, N.Y., 1973, pp. 19–20.

of "employment creation" is seen in exactly the opposite way from what it is by Keynesian-minded economists.

We referred above to *population growth* as a factor that renders difficult the interpretation of experience. In countries like Rhodesia and the Republic of South Africa, we believe, it has prevented what would have been an unprecedented rate of improvement in the living standards of the black races, and hence of their cultural development and political advancement. Of course, the Blacks have been confined to sub-optimal production through the white labor unions' monopolization of skilled and responsible work.[18] But, especially in the "border areas" and in the "homelands," the barriers have been weakening for nearly two decades. The benefits for the Blacks have, however, been largely obscured by reason of rising survival rates. The Blacks of working age have multiplied much more rapidly than the Whites, reducing the market-clearing value of their labor.

Immigration, legal or illegal, and migrant labor are also important factors influencing the real value of employment outlets, including sub-optimal outlets. But growing population, through both natural increase and immigration, is not a simple phenomenon. It is never easy to interpret the economic adage, "With each new mouth there comes a new pair of hands."

---

[18] The monopolization, mainly enforced through the Wage Act and insistence on "the rate for the job," has constituted the principal color bar in Southern Africa. "Job reservation" restraints, although exposing the original spirit of apartheid (i.e., before it was gradually refashioned during the last two decades as "separate development"), have at all times been of *relatively* minor importance. See W. H. HUTT, *Economics of the Colour Bar,* Institute of Economic Affairs, London, 1964.

Chapter I

Definition of Idleness

1

Similar causes exist for idleness in
labor, equipment and all other resources

The object of this essay is to remove certain common
confusions concerning the significance of idle productive resources. We shall endeavor to do so by the introduction of a new set of concepts and definitions. The problems
at issue are generally referred to as those of "surplus
capacity" in the case of equipment and "unemployment" in
the case of labor. Similar causes of the different phenomena
of idleness are, we shall argue, active in both cases.[1] Indeed,
so true and important does this contention seem to be, that
practically all recent attempts to analyze realistically the
nature and causes of unemployment of labor have, we
believe, gone seriously astray through failure to recognize
it; or at any rate they appear to have been led into error
through the necessary crudeness of attempts to deal with

---

[1] But to recognize this truth is to lay ourselves open to the ever-recurring
jibe about a philosophy which tolerates a market in which human life is
bought and sold!

attributes common to all types of productive resources by considering their manifestation in one type only.[2] In the case of purely natural resources, no "problems" of idleness are usually regarded as arising, although the more careful economists have recognized that "produced" and "non-produced" resources are governed by the same laws of utilization. We shall, then, deal with the various conceptions of idleness of resources in general.

2

Idleness has one appearance but exists in several senses

We can define *idleness* in several ways. That is, we can use the term in various senses. Different causes produce idleness of different types and significance. Our main thesis is that confusion arises from a failure to recognize the consequences of this obvious truth. When there is a plurality of conditions each of which in its pure state has a *similar appearance,* and each of which has its own cause, what appears to be a simple quality may in fact be a mixture of quite separate attributes. Unemployment or idleness may exist in several different senses while all the states, in their "pure" form, may look alike.[3] How serious the confusion can be will be realized when it is remembered that what

---

[2] This particular source of possible confusion is most marked in the work of Keynes and his interpreters. Keynes' analysis is made to depend upon an *Aggregate Demand Function* in which demand means "the proceeds which *entrepreneurs* expect to receive from the employment of N men." (*General Theory of Employment, Interest, and Money,* p. 25.) For completeness, he needs further functions in which demand means the proceeds which *entrepreneurs* expect to get from the employment of so many units of equipment, or other resources.

[3] E.g., in the case of a machine, its wheels may not be turning; but the significance of that fact may be any one of many things.

constitutes idleness from one point of view may be utilization from another. Keynes has attempted (and his interpreters have followed in his footsteps) to simplify and give unity to the conception of unemployment of *labor* by using a definition of "disutility" which lumps together many quite different things.[4] He defines "disutility" as covering "every kind of reason which might lead a man, or a body of men, to withhold their labor rather than accept a wage which had to them a utility below a certain minimum."[5] Now this definition draws a veil over many of the issues which we have to face. We shall show that the significance of withheld labor can be classed into at least six vitally distinct categories, the nature of the unemployment being radically different in each case.

3

The necessity for definition

The analysis of *idleness* calls therefore for the isolation and definition of the various states which that broad term covers. But new definitions are irritating things, and the mere process of multiplying terms may appear to be both pretentious and barren. If we determine to have a new definition, said Malthus, "in every case where the old one is not quite complete, the chances are that we shall subject the science to all the serious disadvantages of a frequent change of terms without finally accomplishing our object."[6] Neverthe-

---

[4] In Mr. R. F. Harrod's treatment the term "disutility" is at first used in an unobjectionable way, that is, when it is used to explain output (other than leisure) under Crusoe conditions. But when he jumps from this to the notion of "inducement to work," which embodies the parallel force in society (*The Trade Cycle,* p. 10), all our objections hold.

[5] KEYNES, op. cit., p. 6.

[6] MALTHUS, *Definitions in Political Economy,* p. 6.

less, we feel confident that the terms here proposed *do* qualify under Malthus's common-sense exception, namely, that "a change would be beneficial and decidedly contribute to the advancement of the science."[7] And we have tried to adhere to "the fundamental principle" which Gustav Cassel has laid down. "The introduction of definitions," he says, "should be based on a preliminary scientific analysis of economic reality. When this analysis has shown that a certain economic concept is of essential importance and can be distinguished with sufficient exactness, the time has come for giving a name to this concept, that is to say, for introducing a new definition."[8]

4

*Popular conceptions of unemployment
of labor recognized by custom and law do not
help us to define "idleness"*

But to analyze "economic reality" does not mean that we should try to make our conceptions harmonize with those based on popular usage, when that usage is confused. Even if popular but confused conceptions have been given recognition by custom or law we can seldom usefully adopt them. Thus, Professor Pigou's attempt to handle unemployment by defining "desire to be employed" as "desire to be employed at current rates of wages,"[9] and by regarding unemployment as the absence of employment at that rate, is an attempt which, in spite of its *intended* realism, dodges instead of encounters the difficulties of the subject. It is

---

[7] Ibid., p. 5.

[8] CASSEL, *Economics as a Quantitative Science,* p. 7. See appendix to this chapter on "Definitions."

[9] PIGOU, *Theory of Unemployment,* p. 4.

true that his definition corresponds roughly to an official British view of "suitable employment," the absence of which has been held to constitute unemployment in the legal sense. But if it is made the basis of analysis, all the really fundamental aspects of idleness are passed over. It will be seen, for instance, that under the definitions which we are about to put forward, if capitalist interlopers (e.g., "the bad employers") are offering an unemployed worker £3 10s 0d. a week for a job when the trade-union rate (the "current rate") is £4, and he refuses to accept it out of loyalty to the union's wage policy, it is, in the first place, clearly a case of "withheld capacity," and *also,* in the second place, a case of "participating idleness" or one of "preferred idleness." To ignore these aspects is, we believe, to overlook all the crucial issues.

5
The categories isolated here are based on logical rather than empirical criteria

We shall here distinguish between the following types of idleness: (*a*) idleness of valueless resources; (*b*) pseudo-idleness; (*c*) preferred idleness; (*d*) participating idleness; (*e*) enforced idleness; (*f*) withheld capacity; (*g*) strike idleness; (*h*) aggressive idleness. A state of *utilization* which has been described as "disguised unemployment" in the case of labor, we shall recognize as (*i*) "diverted resources." We believe that every kind of unemployment of resources which has been discussed in the wide literature dealing with unemployment of labor, and in the relatively few contributions which treat of the idleness of other resources, can be included under one or more of these headings. Other terms for the same conditions have been employed, but they have often covered, in a quite unjustifiable way, absolutely different things. Thus, books on the unemployment of labor use the adjectives: "seasonal," "cyclical," "slump," "casual," "frictional," "technological" and so forth. But these descriptions are based on *empirical* rather than *logical* criteria. They are not the "precise conceptions" demanded by Sidgwick's standards for definitions and terms.[10] They will all be found, on analysis, to involve factors which *must* be expressed through the causes set forth above. It will be shown that, although empirical definitions undoubtedly have their appropriateness in particular studies, until they are regarded from the angle demanded by our logical scheme, it is difficult for their true significance to be plain. For in each case one of the factors we have indicated will be seen to be *the proximate cause.* We mean by this that the removal of the one factor would lead to the utilization of the resource, or else to the continued idleness of the resource in some other sense only and from some other cause. In certain cases, more than one of these causes (with its corresponding type of idleness) may be present while the removal of any one would mean the cessation of the others. In *other* cases the causes (and the appropriate types of idleness) are independent.[11]

6
Rational policies must recognize our categories

*   It must be admitted that knowledge of the category into which any type of idleness falls may not always be the most

---

[10] See appendix to this chapter.

[11] Professor Pigou's discussion of the causation of unemployment (ibid., Part I, Chap. VI) seems to overlook what we here regard as fundamental because he apparently conceives of a plurality of causes of a *homogeneous* condition which can be called "unemployment."

important knowledge, but it is *essential* knowledge in every case. Thus, for some discussions, to say that certain resources are idle because they fall into the "valueless resources" category will not be helpful if we stop there. Statesmen and reformers will want to know *why* they are valueless. And discussion of the implications of this condition will therefore bring under examination the determinants of the margin between valuable and valueless resources. Nevertheless, we conceive it to be one of the supreme tasks in the present state of popular (and even academic) controversy to emphasize the consequences of the greater part of deplorable idleness *not* falling into this particular category.[12] We shall demonstrate (*a*) that idleness can be analyzed into logically separate classes, the relation of each of which to the wider conception of "waste" has not been sufficiently discussed; and (*b*) that whatever forces lying deeper in the social organism may be held to be responsible for idleness, in the absence of one or more of the causes that we have defined, the condition would not exist.

7

There can be no measure of utilization or idleness

We shall conceive of "unemployment" or "idleness," in all the different senses that we propose to distinguish, as a

---

[12] The only reference to this basic truth that we have noticed in economic literature is in a recent article by R. F. Kahn. He says, concerning the unrealistic assumption of "full employment" in Professor Pigou's *Economics of Welfare*: "That the existence of uncultivated land does not invalidate the methods and conclusions of the *Economics of Welfare* is sufficiently obvious. That the existence of unemployed labor upsets all these arguments is equally obvious. But in what way labor differs from land is not completely apparent." But Dr. Kahn says that this "is a matter for separate discussion." *Economic Journal*, March 1935, p. 1.

condition or quality. It cannot be thought of quantitatively. In so far as different types of resources can be defined in terms of quantity, it is possible to talk of the amount of resources which are in the condition of being utilized or employed. We can also realistically refer to the proportion of total time, or the proportion of the conventional working days in a year (or some other time standard) during which the services of particular resources (e.g., looms or weavers) are being utilized. But we cannot talk of the amount of employment in any other way. We cannot add together, say, the number of hours of utilization of a locomotive, of the track, and of the signals. Similarly, we cannot aggregate the employment of the engine driver, the fireman, the guard, and the signalman.

8

Keynes' attempt to measure
"employment" has absurd implications

*   But Keynes *does* try to conceive of employment of labor as a measurable condition. He discusses the sum of all the employment involved in all the different occupations of labor, expressed in terms of "men." The only major difficulty that he appears to recognize is that which arises through differences of remuneration; and he thinks that it is sufficient for his purpose to get over the difficulty by "taking an hour's employment of ordinary labor as our unit and weighting an hour's employment of special labor in proportion to its remuneration."[13] In other words, he regards "individuals as contributing to the supply of labor in proportion to their remuneration.[14] Such a definition of employment

---

[13] KEYNES, op. cit., p. 41.
[14] Ibid., p. 42.

must lead to the most absurd results. Thus, if the workers in a trade can organize and drive 10 percent of their number into inferior occupations, reduce by 10 percent the amount of labor supplied, and in so doing increase the aggregate earnings of that trade by, say, 20 percent, then the proportion of all employment enjoyed by them and the proportion of the total labor supplied by them must be regarded as increased! Apparently this is so in spite of "the level of employment," N, being expressed in terms of "men." Curiously enough, Keynes recognizes that "the community's output of goods and services is a nonhomogeneous complex which cannot be measured . . .";[15] he sees that there is no solution of the "problem of comparing one real output with another";[16] and he is clearly aware of the connected difficulty arising out of the vagueness of the "price level concept."[17] But by substituting the notion of "employment" he has not escaped the impossibility of defining aggregate output. For, if different sorts of "employment" are regarded as having values, are we not really thinking of them as the output of services? What else *can* be valued? And one can no more measure "employment" in the sense of the output of productive services in general than one can the output of consumers' goods and consumers' services in general to which they lead. Yet the whole of Keynes' general the-

---

[15] Ibid., p. 38.

[16] Ibid., p. 39. Keynes' disciples have not all followed him here. Thus, Mr. R. F. HARROD talks of "the level of output as a whole," and even of "the equilibrium level of output of the community as a whole." *The Trade Cycle*, pp. 13, 30.

[17] Keynes qualifies his position in an obscure way when he says that these difficulties "are 'purely theoretical' in the sense that they never perplex, or indeed enter in any way into, business decisions and have no relevance to the causal sequence of economic events, which are clear-cut and determinate in spite of the quantitative indeterminacy of these concepts." Op. cit., p. 39.

ory, developed "with a princely profusion of reasoning,"[18] is erected on an "Aggregate Supply Function" which assumes that "employment" so conceived *can* be measured. The function (expressed as $Z = \varphi N$, N being a level of employment induced by an expectation of a return, Z) hides what may possibly be a serious fallacy in the apparent definiteness of an equation. In avoiding the use of the meaningless term "output," he has not avoided the concept itself. For N is nothing but output at an early stage of production. His weighting leaves no meaning in the unit "men" at all. We cannot, as he assumes, "aggregate the N's in a way which we cannot aggregate the O's[19] (O being an output). ΣN is no more a numerical quantity than ΣO. We shall here assume that all such attempts to devise a logically tenable quantitative concept of utilization or employment are misconceived. This assumption will in no way hinder the sort of analysis of the problem which we conceive to be realistic and useful.

9
Orthodox theory does not,
as has been alleged, assume "full employment"

*   Keynes also alleges that classical and orthodox theory "is best regarded as a theory of distribution of conditions of full employment"[20] (apparently because some writers have assumed "full employment" as a methodological device in abstract analysis). His assertion has subsequently been emphasized and repeated by several writers who have been impressed by this startling revelation. And the "man in

---

[18] R. F. HARROD, op. cit., p. 120.

[19] KEYNES, op. cit., p. 45.

[20] Ibid., p. 16.

the street," who is also anxious to believe that orthodox economists have been astonishingly stupid, has been pleased to find his predilections confirmed. We believe, however, that the types of idleness analyzed in the pages which follow are all of a kind which are implicit—if not expressed in sufficiently clear terms—in orthodox teaching. This essay is felt to be original only in the sense that, through more careful definition, it seeks to clarify what is already known and understood. It is pure orthodoxy, as we understand that term. But it nowhere assumes the absence of the conditions it discusses. Keynes says that since Malthus there has been a "lack of correspondence between the results of (the professional economists') theory and the facts of observation."[21] Under our own interpretation of their writings that has not been so. And the present discussion obviously recognizes the continuous and necessary existence in society of idle resources in many different senses. It may be that the classical economists overlooked many important aspects of demand in a dynamic economy. But they were realists, and their discussions imply an awareness of aspects of utilization to which their modern critics appear to be blind. Certainly the important issues here dealt with have not been faced in recent controversies.

10
"Full employment" has no meaning as an absolute condition

As a matter of fact, it will be an implication of our subsequent analysis that the notion of "full employment" *as an absolute condition* can have no meaning. Given some basic ideal, e.g., consumers' sovereignty, any particular resource

---

[21] Ibid., p. 33.

may be said to be *under*employed" or "idling" when that ideal would be better served by the transfer of resources from other uses to cooperate with it. It would be "fully employed" in that sense if there would be no advantage in attracting other resources to cooperate with it. But it might then be working very slowly (as compared, say, to its former working). Even if continuously employed, the resources would appear to be "idling"; and yet they would be fully employed in the only rational connotation we can suggest for "full," i.e., as a synonym for *"optimum."*[22] We can conceive of "fuller" employment but not "full" in the sense of "complete." The term "full employment" might also be used in an historical or a comparative sense, to mean the degree of utilization originally expected, or achieved at a former period, or realized in similar resources elsewhere. But it is clear that none of those writers who use the term have such comparisons in mind.

11
"Idling," meaning
"underemployment," is a parallel conception to "idleness"

The conception of "idling" is allied to that of "idleness." The former is partial, the latter is absolute. In each of the senses of "idleness" distinguished in paragraph 5, there is a parallel conception of *"idling."* It means "underemployment." Thus, many productive instruments may be used intensively or extensively. A machine may work at various speeds, for instance. It may be used, say in the production

---

[22] The conception of "full employment" *in general* is that of a "wasteless economy." It excludes the possibility of "diverted resources" as well as all forms of nonproductive idleness. For the meaning of "diverted resources" see Chap. IX, paras. 3 and 4.

of one hundred articles a day either by being operated for the whole of the conventional day of eight hours, or by being operated at twice that speed, producing the same output in four hours and standing idle for the other four hours. From some points of view, the position is identical in these two cases. But in this exposition we shall concentrate on the condition of "idleness." All that can be said about its significance applies with equal relevance to "idling." And "idleness" is a distinguishable, indisputable and absolute attribute common to many different states.

12
Criteria for definition

This essay might be described as a study in definition. Now there have always been those who were impatient of the process of meticulous definition. Richard Jones, Auguste Comte and Thorold Rogers as well as Malthus are mentioned by J. N. Keynes as having held that concentration on definition is pedantic and useless. "Political economy is said to have strangled itself with definitions."[23] Some explanation or defense of our method of basing an analysis of idleness upon careful definition may therefore be called for. Of course, this essay is itself an obvious defense of the method, but the pronouncements of the logicians of economic science may also be relied upon. J. N. Keynes himself has not agreed with the writers he quotes. He says, "There is nothing arbitrary or unessential in *analyzing the precise content of a notion* in the various connections in which it is involved."[24] Cairnes, indeed, seemed to envisage the neces-

---

[23] J. N. KEYNES, *Scope and Method of Political Economy*, p. 153.
[24] Ibid., p. 156 (our italics).

sity for *constant* redefinition. "Students of the social sciences," he said, "must be prepared for the necessity of constantly modifying their classifications and, by consequence, their definitions . . ."[25] And in endeavoring "to make our conceptions as precise as possible,"[26] we feel that we have been able to illustrate, in an important field, Sidgwick's observations that "reflective contemplation is naturally stimulated by the effort to define"[27] and that as *much— if not more—importance attaches to the process of defining as to the resulting definition itself.* We have tried also, in the analysis which follows, to avoid the "formal definitions" of which Cannan disapproved, in the sense in which he disapproved of them; for we have taken heed of his other warning and endeavored to avoid "the formation of an economic language understood only by specialists."[28] Such new terms as we have introduced should be immediately comprehensible by the layman. The term "participating idleness" gave trouble, but Cannan would surely have approved of it. And, further, an attempt has been made to adhere to the rule that Cairnes quoted from J. S. Mill, namely, that in the nomenclature of definitions "the aids of derivation and analogy" should be "employed to keep alive a consciousness of all that is signified by them."[29] This applies, we believe, even to our original but seemingly highly important conception of "participating idleness" as well as to the vaguely recognized conceptions that we have

[25] J. E. CAIRNES, *Character and Logical Method of Political Economy,* p. 146.

[26] H. SIDGWICK, *Political Economy,* p. 62.

[27] Ibid., p. 60.

[28] *Palgrave's Dictionary.* Article on "Definition."

[29] J. S. Mill, quoted in CAIRNES, op. cit., p. 151.

termed "pseudo-idleness" and "aggressive idleness." But in choosing terms for our definitions, we have not been able to make use of Malthus' suggestion that, in introducing distinctions which cannot be described by "terms which are of daily occurrence," the next best authority is that of the "most celebrated writers in the science."[30] For, strange as it may seem, our "celebrated writers" have never specifically analyzed idleness in the very simple but apparently basic way that is here attempted. Hence it has been quite impossible to avoid this attempt to burden economic science with new terms.

---

[30] MALTHUS, *Definitions in Political Economy,* pp. 4–5.

Appendix

Notes and Comments on Chapter I

In the reference to "the margin between valuable and valueless resources" (paragraph 6) we could usefully **6** have called attention at this stage to the process under which *potential* assets become *actual* assets *passively*. Particular resources acquire value simply through an increase in demand for them and, *in general,* through growth in the flow of noncompeting inputs and outputs. Some aspects of this process are discussed in Chapter II, paragraphs 1 to 6. The process of *production* can be seen as "the creation of value," which (as we mentioned in the Introduction, p. 35) is J. B. Say's definition of "production" whether the value is created accidentally, passively, or as the result of purposeful action).[1] It can be best envisaged as the flow of productive services rendered by men or assets. But that is also "income." Income is generated by production and by nothing else.

---

[1] The extermination of value in assets (again according to Say's definition) is "consumption" (whether the "extermination" is purposeful, accidental or passive—e.g., through a transfer of consumer preference).

8   In showing, in paragraph 8, that the "employment" of men and assets is nothing more than the supply of their "services," it would have improved communication had we pointed out that such services, unless consumed as they are rendered, are "inputs," embodied in a stock of assets which is in process of concurrent consumption (extermination of value). The flow of services (purposely or passively produced) replaces, partly or wholly, or more than replaces, the value of the accompanying consumption, in the latter case adding to the value of the assets stock. Hence, rigorously defined, "employment," "production" and "income" are identical concepts both as processes and as magnitudes.

We can of course talk of the "utilization" of assets and the "employment" of men, but for most purposes it is better to use one term to cover both. The condition can be measured only in terms of the *value* of productive services provided. The full flow of heterogeneous productive services and inputs (income) is measurable not only in terms of dollars or other actual money units but (subject to all the conceptual difficulties involved in price averages) in terms of abstractly conceived money units of "constant purchasing power" (i.e., in "real terms"). It is, as we have shown, hardly meaningfully measurable in "physical terms."

9, 10   It seems to us now that, in paragraphs 9 and 10, the only notion of *"full* employment" in the economy as a whole which has meaning is that condition which would be experienced under the imaginary circumstances in which all prices (both of inputs and outputs) are fixed at predicted market-clearing values. Such abstractly envisaged circumstances are not to be regarded as "ideal." Many workers, and the complementary assets they use, may be "fully employed" in "sub-optimal" employments (i.e., in what we term, in the text, "disguised unemployment" or "diverted capacity." See pp. 47, 183–85). The complementary assets to labor will then become *specialized* for less productive forms of activity —"sub-optimal" forms.

In the case of nonversatile equipment supplied by an entrepreneur in the expectation of a yield in excess of interest on each increment of investment in it, while that expectation is not fully realized, the equipment may be regarded as "fully employed" in the sense explained in the above paragraph, even when the *actual* returns to the capital devoted to it do not fully cover interest. In such a case there will have been some capital consumption, some "extermination of value," unless a recovery is predicted in demand for the services of the assets or unless a fall in complementary costs is predicted. Minimization of such a loss *may* require, however, just as much investment in complementary inputs (e.g., in labor) as was originally planned for.

Chapter II

Valueless Resources

1

*Valueless idle resources are those which
it would not pay any individual to employ,
even if no charge were made for their use*

The first form of idleness, we have termed "valueless   *
resources." Two conditions might be understood by
this term: firstly, resources of no capital value; secondly,
resources which at any time it would not pay any individual
to employ for any purpose, even if no charge were made
for their use.[1] We shall adopt the second meaning as some
resources may be usefully regarded as temporarily valueless; and some resources may have no capital value or a
negative capital value, and yet provide valuable services
and be valuable in our sense. It is easy to illustrate the conception in the case of natural resources. Orthodox economics has at all times recognized that there exists a huge
amount of unemployed natural resources of this type, more
and more of which, with developing technique and expand-

---

[1] The phrase "even if no charge were made for their use" covers all but one
unimportant special case discussed below (para 11).

ing population, have been observed firstly, to be drawn into active exploitation; and secondly, when they are scarce, to acquire capital value. Much unoccupied land falls into this category. Another example is that of the tides which are a source of immense potential power which it seldom pays, at present, to exploit. Equipment, and even the powers of human beings, *can* be conceived of as falling under the heading of "valueless resources," although it is less easy to think of instances.

2

The range of valuable resources may expand or contract

Resources may be employed but valueless. Uncongested rivers, and oceans, and the air that we breathe, may be regarded as examples. No scarcity, or an infinitesimal scarcity attaches to the services of marginal resources in such cases. No social problem arises, as Hume pointed out in 1751,[2] in respect of the utilization of productive powers of this kind. If they are not employed, it is clearly because cooperant resources can be better employed elsewhere. They make no claim on the value of what is produced. But the more important examples of utilized but valueless resources are to be found where economic change is tending to confer value on them; and they are important because of the light which they throw upon the nature of the employment of resources which lie *within* the range of valuable resources. The case of land is clearest because we can conceive of the range in terms of the economically arbitrary notion of area. But the conception of a boundary or margin

---

[2] HUME, *An Inquiry Concerning the Principles of Morals,* opening of Chap. III, part (i) "Of Justice."

within which resources have some value and outside of which they are without value can apply to all resources, although there can be no idea of measurement of the range so imagined. The position of this boundary may change: it may be extended or it may be drawn in. That is, the compass of resources possessing *some* scarcity may vary.

3
The range of valuable resources
does not reflect the effectiveness of the response
to consumers' (or some other) sovereignty

Such variations are of importance in studies of idleness; but it must be recognized that they do not indicate the extent to which the preferences of the community are receiving the most effective satisfaction. In other words, variations in the range of valuable resources do not correspond in any certain way with any of the conceptions to which different definitions of social or national income have attempted to give concreteness. As we have already argued, there can be no criterion of the size of production as a whole. The conception of the effectiveness of response to consumers' sovereignty or some other sovereignty, a response which is not subject to numerical measurement, is the only logically satisfactory criterion of effective production. We make this point at this stage in order to emphasize the error of the very likely assumption that, if the range of valuable resources happens to contract, it is *necessarily* a phenomenon to be deplored. The point may be illustrated by consideration of the case of an increased demand for leisure, which is one of the causes of what has been termed a "decreased propensity to consume." Although, *ceteris paribus,* some physical resources *tend to* lose value in such a case,[3] the result itself is in no sense to be regretted in the light of the consumers' sovereignty ideal. On the other hand, if there is a similar decreased willingness to cooperate through exchange, owing to a collusive (or State enforced) reduction of the hours of labor, with work-sharing intention, there will be a similar tendency for some cooperant physical resources to lose value (and perhaps to fall valueless) in a manner which *does* conflict with the ideal. It is probable that most withholdings of capacity (through price or wage-rate fixations, output restrictions, or other protections of private income rights) have the effect of causing the range of valuable resources to contract; and it is only when these policies are the origin of such idleness that there is any social loss reflected.[4]

4

The vague phrase "increase in economic activity"
can only have meaning if it refers to a fall in the proportion
of valuable idle resources to all valuable resources

The question of the position of the margin between valuable and valueless resources may be important for some purposes but it is obviously not the problem with which those writers who use phrases like "an increase in the general level of economic activity" are concerned. If that phrase

---

[3] See below, para. 11.

[4] One can conceive of circumstances in which resources as a whole could fall in price without any of them falling *valueless;* and it is even possible for the range of valuable resources to increase while the general tendency is for prices to fall. E.g., in the case of land, technical inventions might confer value on land which was formerly outside the margin but at the same time cause the aggregate value of land to fall. That is, the inventions could render the poorer types of land relatively valuable.

is taken to mean an improvement in the efficiency with which consumers' preferences (or some other sovereignty) are being satisfied, it has no obvious relation to this margin. If, on the other hand, that phrase means a fall in the proportion between resources which have value but are idle and all resources which have value, it does have some meaning, although most abstractions of the nature of "general levels" are dangerous.

5
Purely valueless equipment can have no net scrap value

In the case of equipment, the definition of "valueless resources" is not as easy as with the "gifts of nature." We have the complication that the idle resources may have a net positive scrap value although no immediate hire value. (We can define "scrapping" as the process of destroying specialization.) *Equipment* of a given degree of specialization may be thought of as valueless when it would not pay any individual to use it, for any purpose, even if no charge *greater than the interest on its net positive scrap value were made.* But, *ceteris paribus,* equipment *will* be scrapped when its net positive scrap value exceeds its specialized value. *Purely* valueless equipment can exist only when the costs of scrapping are greater than the scrap is expected to realize.

6
Resources are not valueless because
the costs of depreciation cannot be earned

The fact that, in any instance, depreciation might not be covered if a particular piece of equipment were employed in production (i.e., if the earnings did not cover the sum required to maintain its original physical state) would not bring it into the valueless resources category. To permit a machine to wear out may be socially (or privately) the most profitable way of scrapping it. The excess of its immediate hire value above the interest on its net value as realized material or parts can be regarded as reflecting the immediate specialized value of its services.

7
Idle unscrapped resources possessing scrap value may be in pseudo-idleness

*   But if a plant whose services are valueless in this sense (i.e., as specialized resources), yet has a positive net scrap value, is allowed to remain unscrapped, then its continued idle existence may be due to the fact that it is waiting for an expected revival of demand or an expected fall in costs.[5] If these expectations alone account for its continued idle existence, it falls into a different category which we shall explain later, namely, "pseudo-idleness." We use this term for the case in which the supposedly idle resources *do* have scrap or other market value. They are in "pseudo-idleness" when they are being productively withheld from some other use, "scrapping" being one of these other uses.

8
Idle resources with capital value but no scrap or hire value are "temporarily valueless"

*   If equipment has no positive net scrap value *and* no immediate hire value, while it still has capital value, it must be regarded as *temporarily valueless*. Of course, its capital

---

[5] This is simply a special case of the general position which exists when the present hire value of unscrapped plant is less than the interest obtainable on the capital realizable from scrapping.

value reflects expectations, not prophecy; and the word "temporarily" merely implies an individual's estimate.

9
The idleness of equipment is seldom due to its being purely valueless

The practical implications of these considerations are important. Cases of *purely valueless* plant and equipment (i.e., whose costs of scrapping are estimated to be greater than the value of the scrap),[6] seem hardly likely to be frequent, although exhausted mines and derelict jetties on silted rivers are clear examples. With railways and other public utilities, instances are *imaginable,* but very difficult to discover in practice. Common-sense observation suggests that the condition is virtually nonexistent in the idle plant and equipment which we occasionally contemplate in the industrial world. It always seems that in any price situation in our present experience, there is hardly any specialized plant in the industrial system that an *entrepreneur* (protected from the coercive power which monopoly confers on others) could not use profitably if he were allowed free access to it; if, that is, no charge for hire entered into his costs. Moreover, we believe that the "most profitable" use would seldom involve scrapping, the destruction of specialized capacity.

10
Full utilization of existing resources is more likely to cause the range of valuable resources to expand than to contract

But such an empirical judgment may be misleading, for   *

[6] The presence of this condition alone obviously does not make resources valueless. It is simply one necessary condition. If it is absent, valuelessness is not present.

it is based on the assumption of the continuance of the existing price situation. If our economic system permitted the community to make full use[7] of available resources, the existing price situation would *not* remain. The effect might conceivably be that in any representative case the cheapening of the product through the full utilization of all available resources would exterminate a large part of the value of much equipment, and so cause it to be realized as scrap or, if it were highly specialized, to push it into the category of valueless resources. But we can hardly assume with confidence that this would happen more often than not if the full capacity in *many* individual industries were utilized. And even if it were likely to happen, it does not follow that the *general* release of productive power would have this effect; for the manifold fields of profitable employment of resources when their services are cheap, and the growing diversity of consumers' preferences which can be expected to result (from economies achieved in realizing ends which we are already able to satisfy under the present regime)[8] suggest that it is much more likely that the bounds outside of which "valueless resources" lie will be *extended*. Increased "scrapping" might be resorted to, but that does not mean increased idleness. Unless leisure, or other things requiring less of the services of physical resources, happen to be more wanted in consequence of the release of productive power, the willingness to cooperate through exchange will tend to increase and the range of valuable resources to extend.

---

[7] See Chap. I, para. 10, for conception of "full employment."

[8] For the prices in one industry are costs to a cooperant industry.

11
Resources which have negative capital
value but provide valuable services are unimportant

Resources are not valueless in our sense simply because
the liabilities attached to their possession are equal to or
greater than their value as assets, or because their continued
existence involves costs equal to or greater than the revenues they can earn. Indeed, the resources may be of negative capital value, but still have hire value, and hence be
valuable as resources so long as they exist. Thus, an edifice
like the Eiffel Tower may well cost more to preserve than
the receipts obtainable from its use. It may, nevertheless,
be preserved because, if neglected, it will be a public danger
while the interest on the cost of scrapping it is greater than
the sum required to preserve it. In the meantime, however,
it can provide valuable (i.e., scarce) services. Hence it will
not be valueless in our sense. Again, consider the dumps of
coal mines which are often a nuisance to development. It
has been recently discovered that they can be used for brick
making. Now it is conceivable that in some circumstances
they could be utilized for this purpose provided the manu-
facturer of the bricks was paid a subsidy by the mining
corporation for removing the dumps. Thus, the materials
would be sold at, so to speak, a negative value; but they
would at the same time be valuable resources. Their negative value would be small or large according to whether
the demand for bricks was large or small. It might be more
realistic to regard the material in the dumps as a by-product
of services rendered to the owners of the mine. But the point
which must be made is that the resources would not be
utilized even if no charge was made for their use. The sub-

sidy, or a contract to remove the dumps, would be a necessary condition. The situation arises when resources obtain
value because their utilization enables other costs to be
reduced. It is a special case of joint supply, and of hardly
any practical importance. We have mentioned it for completeness and because it might lead to misconceptions.

12

Except for imbeciles, the sick and children,
there are no parallels to valueless resources in labor

In the case of labor it is even more difficult to conceive of
examples of "valueless resources." Imbeciles and the seriously sick might be regarded as qualifying, in the sense that
there are no means of making their employment profitable.
Convicts, the condition of whose punishment or isolation
makes impracticable their undertaking work in competition
with free labor, fall under this heading also. But if their
services are not utilized because "convict labor" is thought
of as, say, "unfair competition," they cannot be classed as
"valueless resources."[9] Concerning children; although we
are not in the habit of regarding the young as *property,*
there is a sense in which they can be thought of as having
capital value from the outset. Hence, they might be described as "temporarily valueless." Parents, guardians and
society may, however, be observed to be investing in the
young from their birth onward. In *this* situation they are
best thought of as employed; although, as we shall show

---

[9] It is not necessary, as our argument in the previous paragraph made clear,
that the costs of housing, feeding and clothing such convicts should be covered by what they can be made to earn, in order to take them outside the
category of "valueless resources." These costs have to be incurred in any
case.

later, the actual position is often difficult to interpret. When they reach the age at which they are capable of remunerative work (and we know from history that this is a very early age), they may be withheld from the labor market (i), because to enter it would interfere with their education (i.e., the process of investment in them); or (ii), because early employment may destroy their powers and hence the value of their services later; or (iii), because leisure is demanded on their behalf as an end in itself; or (iv), because their unpaid domestic service inside the home is worth more to their parents than they could add to the family earnings from work outside; or finally, (v), because their competition in the labor market is not wanted. In the first and second cases they do not happen to be in the labor market, but they are employed in the sense in which capital equipment in the course of its own production is employed. In part, both cases may be regarded as examples of "pseudo-idleness." In the third case it is a type of "preferred idleness." In the fourth case the children are not idle in any sense. And in the fifth case it is an example of "enforced idleness" or "withheld capacity." The idleness of the very old is usually "preferred idleness" of the leisure kind, but where the receipt of a pension is contingent upon remunerative work not being undertaken, it must be classified as "participating idleness."

13
The "unemployed" are not valueless

If we consider the actual "unemployed," it is impossible to regard them as "valueless resources." They are not unemployed for *that* reason. At low enough wage rates they could practically all be profitably absorbed into some task, even if their earnings were insufficient in many cases to pay for physically or conventionally necessary food, let alone clothing and housing. In a slave economy, such people might be allowed to die off; or they might, for sentimental reasons, be kept alive. But in the latter case, their efforts would still be available and they would not be "valueless resources" so long as the utilization of their efforts produced more than the *extra* outgoings incurred. Imagine a society which decides that a national minimum of subsistence shall be provided for those whose earnings fail to procure a tolerable standard of living (tolerable, that is, in the collective judgment). It is obviously unnecessary in such a society that an individual's earning power shall equal or exceed his freely received allowance in order that his capacity shall be regarded as having positive value. And where philanthropic poor relief exists, the same principle holds. Because a blind man in receipt of services and pocket money equivalent to 30s. a week from a charitable institution can contribute to its funds from the basket making which he is called upon to do a mere 15s. a week, it would be wrong to think of his services as valueless. Thus, both in respect of *capital equipment and labor,* idleness due to absence of value is almost certainly rare and unimportant. That temporary absence of hire value, accompanied by a positive net scrap value which we shall call "pseudo-idleness," is an entirely different sort of condition.

14

*Natural resources which have once
been valuable seldom lose all their value, so that any
subsequent idleness must be due to other causes*

It is not usual for "practical" writers and reformers to think of unexploited *natural* resources as "unemployed."

But they are not essentially different, economically, from labor and *produced* resources. Now it can be observed *as a fact of experience* that once natural resources have acquired value and been utilized or specialized they hardly ever become valueless (*a*) unless their physical nature changes (as under soil erosion or exhaustion, for example); or (*b*) unless they are the refuse from production (mine dumps, for example); or (*c*) unless huge shifts of demand (as from war to peace, for example) take place; or (*d*) unless communities migrate (from exhausted mining districts, for example). In settled communities, the writer can think of very few cases of land going out of cultivation *and* pasturage, except under the coercions or collusions of agricultural "cooperation" and State policy, or where soil exhaustion has destroyed its productive qualities, or under apathetic ownership in the case of "social farms," or where estates are reserved as public or private parks.[10] Still less can instances be found of land, once occupied, losing all capital value; and the *continued*[11] existence of some capital value in such land suggests that in spite of apparent idleness, some services of an income nature are being provided by it. This serves to illustrate further our main point that while it is theoretically conceivable that certain types of labor, capital equipment and once utilized resources can pass outside the margin of profitable employment (when, say, demand is transferred from one set of preferences to another), valueless resources in a "pure" form other than untouched natural resources seem to be rare, and an unimportant type of idleness. The phenomena which reformers deplore when they discuss trade depression are not of this nature.

---

[10] This is a particular case of utilization.

[11] I.e., it cannot be explained as "temporary absence of hire value."

Appendix

Notes and Comments on Chapter II

In paragraph 1, our argument does not deal specifically 1 with a seemingly reasonable objection—namely, that all "resources" must, to be so described, have value: if they are not valuable, they should not be regarded as "resources." Nevertheless, a distinction seems to be necessary: "assets" *must* have value; "resources" *need* not. For instance, the atmosphere and the sun's light and warmth are "resources." But as we have seen valueless resources may become assets.

The *apparent* idleness of valuable resources, discussed in paragraphs 5 and 6, may resemble the passive productivity of inventories of *physically completed* goods of which the 5, 6 productive process is not yet complete. Thus marketing services are inputs incorporated into products, which are not *economically completed* until that has been done. We envisage here the production of time utilities,[1] space util-

---

[1] I.e., carrying goods through time—incurring interest costs, warehousing costs, insurance costs, etc.

ities,[2] availability utilities,[3] assembly utilities,[4] information utilities,[5] etc. These are all services demanded by and supplied to the consumer, their value being incorporated into the final product. The apparent idleness in this case is later to be described (Chapter III, paragraph 1) as *pseudo-*

7 idleness. Paragraph 7 treats of special cases. But we fail to explain, in the text, that "temporarily valueless" resources

8 (referred to in paragraph 8) are also in *"pseudo*-idleness."

10 In paragraph 10, the important point we are making could have been more effectively communicated had we referred explicitly to Say's law of markets. Every release of productive power which had previously been withheld will contribute to the source of demands for all noncompeting inputs and outputs. If, through any form of coercive action costs have been forced up in a wide range of productive operations, so that former rates of investment in inputs become *prospectively* unprofitable (marginal prospective yields falling short of the rate of interest), some already provided fixed assets may be thrown into idleness, with concomitant displacement of complementary labor. The consequential shrinkage of output in any one set of operations means a decline in demands for outputs (and hence for inputs) in some sets of noncompeting operations. It is through the cumulative consequences of pricing inputs and/ or outputs at above market-clearing values that recession is

---

[2] I.e., carrying goods through space, e.g., avocados from California to New York.

[3] E.g., having an avocado ready on the shelves for anybody who should want one at any time.

[4] I.e., having a *range* of goods (e.g., fruit, meat, dairy produce, pet foods, medicine, etc.) available in one store to reduce consumer buying costs.

[5] I.e., informative advertising.

precipitated. For such pricing represses the source of demands as a whole; and it receives its objective expression in a reduced flow of wages, as well as in reduced earnings in the form of interest and profits. That is why what we have called "the general release of productive power" will tend to restore "the willingness to cooperate through exchange" and "the range of valuable resources to extend." The cheapening of any one input or output raises forecast returns from investment in the production of noncompeting outputs generally.

If the reasoning presented in paragraph 10 is acceptable, 10 then surely the claim on the 1939 cover jacket that this book is "largely devoted to criticism of Mr. Keynes' *General Theory*," which Lindley Fraser denied,[6] is not altogether unjustifiable. For the crucial originality of Keynes' *General Theory* was "the unemployment equilibrium thesis," in which it was argued that downward adjustments of input prices fixed above what we have now called "market-clearing levels" would *aggravate* any widespread unemployment of men and assets, and not contribute to the restoration of their employment. Our position is diametrically opposite.

---

[6] See Preface to Second Edition, p. 16.

Chapter III

Pseudo-Idleness

1
Uncompleted equipment in process
of construction must be regarded as employed

How shall we regard productive resources which are in process of being specialized? Surely they must be thought of as employed. The materials in a half-completed ship are no more idle, in any useful sense, than the stocks on which it rests. But this form of employment may be accompanied by other forms of idleness, a possibility of some importance which complicates the position. Uncompleted equipment is only fully employed (in our sense of *optimum* utilization) when investment in it is proceeding at the social *optimum* rate, given existing expectations. Thus, while the vessel *534* which became the *Queen Mary* was actually under construction, the fact that it was not actively earning did not mean that the resources embodied in it were unemployed. But when work on it was stopped because the proposition ceased to be "profitable" to the company owning it—in the light of indications from the ocean freight market—it stood idle in one or more of the other senses which we have to discuss.

2
Individuals adding to their powers through education are employed

We find parallels in the case of labor. The clearest example is in the case of young children. At the outset, they have no usable powers; but as such powers do develop, the most profitable use of them (given contemporary standards of social goodness) is usually their improvement through that form of investment represented by the costs of upbringing and education. And throughout life, when individuals are out of the labor market because the addition to their future hire value from education more than compensates for immediate earnings foregone, they ought properly to be regarded as employed. The determining consideration is whether investment in them is proceeding *at the social optimum rate.* Thus, the raising of the age of voluntary school leaving may have the real object of keeping more juveniles out of the employment market, and it is sometimes quite frankly demanded for this reason. Their condition then obviously partakes of the nature of what we call "withheld capacity" or "enforced idleness" rather than that of being subject to investment. If the standard of schooling available should be such that the juveniles are likely actually to benefit in the long run, then, whatever the motive, the process of investment in them is the explanation of their condition.

3
Individuals conserving their powers through rest are employed

Similar to the case of training is that of the maintenance of physical and mental efficiency in human beings by rest and recuperation. Thus, normal sleeping hours cannot be regarded as idleness; and there is a recuperative (and hence productive) aspect about most leisure.[1] Genuine efficiencies achievable through the mere postponement of children's earnings may conceivably be the best employment of their powers, i.e., irrespective of the education which it incidentally permits.

4
Individuals actively "prospecting"
for remunerative jobs are employed

These specific cases of employment have, however, never been mistaken for unemployment. But other cases falling into the same category have been so mistaken. Thus, a worker in a nonunionized and unprotected trade[2] whose firm closes down in depression may refuse immediately available work in a different job because he feels that to accept it will prevent him from seeking for better openings in his own regular employment or other occupations for which he is peculiarly fitted. Let us for a moment ignore the case in which he is passively waiting and merely preserving his availability. When *actively* searching for work, the situation is that he is really investing in himself by working on his own account without immediate remuneration. He is prospecting. He is doing what he would pay an efficient employment agency to do if the course of politics had allowed that sort of institution to emerge in modern society. He judges that the search for a better opening is worth the risk of immediately foregone income. If his relatives, or his

---

[1] But leisure is, however, usually to be thought of as "preferred idleness."

[2] We make this assumption for simplicity. It avoids the complications referred to in Chaps. VIII–X.

friends, or the State are keeping him then, in a sense, they also may sometimes be regarded as investing in him, and it may still be wrong to think of him as idle. But this condition is very difficult to distinguish *in practice* from the various types of "preferred idleness." Thus, unemployment insurance may lessen his incentive to find work and an apparent or supposed search for the best employment opportunities may be a mask for what is known as "loafing."

5

Pseudo-idleness resembles passive
employment but is not an identical condition

These last examples of employment are seldom treated as employment, but as the workers concerned are serving the community best in their apparent idleness, and as they themselves are remunerated for the service (when their judgment is right—i.e., when their powers have really been guided to employers who can use them most profitably), we ought properly to think of the idleness as spurious. The purpose of this chapter is, however, to draw attention to a *similar* category of employment which is even more easily mistaken for idleness. But it is not quite the same, and we allot to it a separate category which we call "pseudo-idleness." It is a condition which is common and has many forms; and it constitutes a phenomenon of the greatest importance in any study of unemployment of labor, or "surplus capacity" in material resources.

6

Pseudo-idleness exists when the
capital value of resources is greater than their scrap
value, while their net hire value is nil

One of the most common forms of "pseudo-idleness" is

that which exists when resources are being retained in their specialized form (i.e., not being scrapped) because the productive service of carrying them through time is being performed. This condition exists when their capital value is greater than their net positive scrap value, while their immediate hire value is nil. This last phrase may require some explanation. Resources must be reckoned as of "no-hire value" even if they can be hired out but (i), the price obtainable is insufficient to cover depreciation and loss of specialization, *and* (ii), there is a greater *consequent* loss or a smaller *consequent* gain to capital value. That is, we must conceive of a net hire value equal to gross hire value minus depreciation. For when depreciation is not covered, the supposed hire price in part covers the realization of resources as scrap. Thus, suppose expectations concerning the revival of demand to remain unchanged, then, for a piece of equipment to be in "pseudo-idleness," it *is* necessary that an *entrepreneur* should be unable to utilize it profitably while *maintaining its physical efficiency*. The proceeds of the complementary use must be insufficient to finance depreciation in order to bring it into the socially productive category which we call "pseudo-idleness."

7
The service rendered by resources in pseudo-idleness is that of "availability"

Thus, the essence of pseudo-idleness is the preservation of *availability*. For example, in a Communist country, a seaside hotel run for foreigners might become the free abode of the local poor during the "off-season"; but if the resulting dilapidations and costs of supervision could not be covered by some small charge, then the best employment of the building would be to close it down. Such a condition would be socially productive,[3] and it could therefore be brought under this heading. Another example is that of a piece of building land which is kept vacant in anticipation of site scarcity in subsequent years. It is obvious also that, in any given state of knowledge and institutions, there are resources which perform their most wanted services through their mere passive existence—the service of "availability." The resources concerned might be capable of being hired out for certain other purposes, but they would then *directly* lose their availability for some special task (which *entrepreneurs* are prepared to bet will be wanting their services later). Hence their present utilization comes to be regarded as likely to bring about a more than countervailing loss in capital value. The loss of availability is a particular case of loss of specialization. Applying our definition in paragraph 6, therefore, they should be rightly regarded as of no immediate net *hire* value.

8

Pseudo-idleness can be illustrated in capital consumers' goods and capital producers' goods

The simplest illustrations of the productive service of mere availability seem almost fatuous. Consider capital consumers' commodities of occasional utilization like the Gramophone which is played only at odd times, the silk hat which is worn only at weddings and funerals, or the picture which is only providing obvious "satisfactions" when it is actually looked at. To refer to these as in "pseudo-idleness" may appear ironical. But closely parallel cases clearly involve

---

[3] Assuming, of course, that the hypothetical Communist government was trying to give recognition to the consumers' sovereignty ideal.

problems of some importance. Thus, I may have a dozen suits of clothes, three cars (two of which are always in the garage), and so forth. One obvious aspect of all these things is that they are purchased "to be available." A good deal of plant in the industrial world is also in this state. It exists because from time to time it will happen to be wanted. The most indubitable cases in the field of *producers'* goods are those in which the phenomenon of "pseudo-idleness" has some regular periodicity. Thus, the plant of a salmon canning factory will not be working out of season, but it will not be unproductive because of that. Ploughs and harvesting machinery may have no alternative uses until the return of the appropriate season. The bottling apparatus of a jam factory may be still for the early hours of each conventional working day. Such regular, recurrent idleness can be confidently classed as "pseudo-idleness." Spasmodic "pseudo-idleness," on the other hand, can often be distinguished from idleness in other senses only with much uncertainty.

9

"Availability" may be regarded as continuously
purchased in the form of capital investment until
utilization takes place, or as continuously enjoyed
and consumed in the form of income

The net loss of income from resources in pseudo-idleness may be regarded as the cumulative investment of an unrealized income. A sum equal to the interest on the scrap value can be thought of as being continuously invested in the resources. Considered from this angle, it must obviously be believed that from such a cumulative investment a return will some day be forthcoming. This unrealized income and investment aspect is present in many cases of "pseudo-idle-

ness." The ends of production seem to be better served if
productive resources (which can wear out or otherwise be
consumed with use, or which can be specialized into other
forms) are kept for purposes which *entrepreneurs* are pre-
purchased as capital. In other cases, the availability itself
pared to bet will be *more* wanted later.[4] "Availability" is
is more realistically regarded as the income. Thus, all my
unutilized consumers' capital goods in my home, from my
radio set to my telephone and fire extinguisher, bring me
continuous satisfactions simply through my knowledge that
they are there. Or again, the armaments of a country in time
of peace also supply a service in the threat which their
existence implies to foreign powers. And we cannot say that
a fire station has provided no services in a month in which
there have been no fires.

10
*The purchase of availability is taking place,
even when it is preserved without actual idleness*

Resources may, however, be held up for some more
wanted employment in such a way that they are not actually
idle. The process of investment in them, or of continuous
receipt of "availability" services is still present. But the
resulting condition of the resources is seldom regarded as
idleness; it cannot be very appropriately described as
"pseudo-idleness"; and it can hardly be usefully termed
"pseudo-diverted resources,"[5] although that term suggests
its real category. Thus, the building land kept vacant in
anticipation of site scarcity (which we have just considered

---

[4] The most common cause of such a situation is an expected revival of demand or an expected fall in costs.

[5] See Chap. IX., paras. 3 and 4.

in this connection) might be employed and bring in some income in the meantime by being used as a car park or as a playing field. It is then performing a *double function;* it is giving day-to-day services *and* it is preserving its availability or "mobility." Whenever resources are withheld from immediately more profitable specialization or despecialization because of expectations of a different situation in the future, a productive service is being performed. When this service is expressed in its pure or simple form, it constitutes the "pseudo-idleness" that we have defined.

11

The indivisibility of an efficient unit of specialized equipment is a common cause of pseudo-idleness under fluctuating or spasmodic demand

One of the most important causes of "pseudo-idleness" in the modern industrial system is what has been called "the technical factor," combined with specialization. That is, the efficient unit of equipment in relation to the relevant market for the product may be large while its appropriate output may be small. This is sometimes referred to in abstract discussion as the quality of "indivisibility." The essence of the situation is that the capital cost of the "indivisible" plant may not be negligible in comparison with all costs, while the equipment itself is only occasionally, or partially, utilized. A most obvious example of this is to be found in the petrol supply apparatus provided by *competing* retailers of that commodity. The services of the equipment they possess may, in sparse districts, be actually demanded for a small proportion of the day or week only. But if the relations of the retailers are truly competing, the occasionally used equipment represents no waste or unwanted duplication. It is continuously providing the service of "availability." Obviously, therefore, under an "advanced" system of specialization of resources, that is, under a highly developed "roundaboutness" in productive processes, there is likely to be a relatively large extent of "pseudo-idleness" in equipment. But there is no inherent waste involved. The economies of "roundaboutness" in industry may, of course, involve continuous "scrapping" as an alternative to recurrently or spasmodically idle plant; and it is a crude (although common) error to suppose that either "pseudo-idleness" or "scrapping" is evidence of the wasteful use of resources.

12

Indivisibility may also cause pseudo-idleness under constant demand

But pseudo-idleness may also be present under constant demand for the equipment's service. It is, however, much less important than the cases which arise under fluctuating or spasmodic demand. We have seen that "full employment" is a relative conception. That is, a piece of indivisible equipment is fully employed when other resources cannot be usefully (e.g., from the standpoint of consumers' sovereignty) diverted from other occupations to cooperate with it. When there is a fluctuating demand, the extent of "full employment" varies inversely with pseudo-idleness; and when there is a constant demand, there may be physical idleness for, say, a constant part of the working day, which may also fall into the pseudo-idleness category. The condition can arise when the unit of equipment can provide more services than it is economic to utilize, while it is impossible to obtain at all, or impossible to obtain except at a higher cost, a smaller piece of equipment providing fewer services. The test for the simplest case of pseudo-idleness under constant demand is this: Has the equipment a net positive hire value during the idle periods? If it *has,* the "surplus capacity" is presumably "withheld capacity" and not in "pseudo-idleness." But the apparent withholding will be spurious if some productive function is performed by the exclusion of cooperant resources during the idle period. In that case, the "surplus capacity" will still be describable as in "pseudo-idleness."[6] We shall deal with this case (which is probably of hardly any practical importance) in Chapter X, paragraph 13.

13

Reserves of goods in course of
liquidation may be in pseudo-idleness

Most stocks of goods for sale, but not all, must be thought of as in "pseudo-idleness." Consumers' goods, for instance, are clearly being distributed over time in accordance with consumers' demand. The criterion of absence of immediate hire value is not obvious here. But we can make use of the same principle through the rule that the balance of a "surplus" of consumers' goods (accumulated through seasonal supply and continuous demand, or continuous supply and seasonal demand, or a fortuitously accumulated "surplus")[7] is in a state of "pseudo-idleness" when its rate of liquidation

---

[6] The same applies, in the abstract, to pseudo-idleness under fluctuating demand. It is most clearly illustrated under the constant demand assumption.

[7] But accumulated stocks may often represent "withheld capacity" and *conceivably* even other forms of idleness, e.g., "aggressive idleness." See W. H. HUTT, "Nature of Aggressive Selling," in *Economica,* August 1935, pp. 312 *et seq.*

is being determined by expectation of the future demand and supply position as modified by the costs of holding. The most important case of this is that of stocks which are in the nature of a "reserve" to meet the vagaries of day-to-day or week-to-week demand. Consider consumers' goods held in the course of the marketing process, e.g., the stocks kept in a retail shop. The consumer *pays* for their availability. The mere presence of the goods in that place is the performance of a productive function, sometimes called by writers on marketing "the function of assembly." Thus, those who occasionally wear silk hats will actually purchase them on unpredictable occasions. Yet they will expect them to be available in the shop when they chance to require them. To secure availability, therefore, reserves will be necessary. When this condition applies to consumers' goods, however, it is never thought of as involving any problem by practical people. But it is quite important, nevertheless, for the same phenomenon receives manifestations in the field of producers' goods (capital goods) and is then more frequently regarded as idleness than recognized as utilization.

Appendix

Notes and Comments on Chapter III

In explaining, in paragraph 4, that the worker who is actively "prospecting" for the best available employment outlets is not properly to be regarded as "unemployed," we should have explained that his role is then essentially entrepreneurial. He is searching for the most productive and remunerative uses for his efforts and skills, including those jobs which he judges have the most favorable prospects. Like all entrepreneurs, he is remunerated by a profit when (through acumen, pertinacity and/or good luck) he is successful in finding a post in which the remuneration he accepts is at least sufficient to compensate for his costs of prospecting (mainly, the sacrifice of sub-optimal remuneration forgone). Similarly, he is penalized by a loss when (through poor judgment or bad luck) he would have been better off if he had accepted an available sub-optimal job earlier.

It must not be assumed that the sacrifice of currently available sub-optimal earnings is *necessary* for the prospecting or job-search process to be performed. Employed persons also can and very often do devote some of their leisure to searching for more remunerative or more pleasant occupations. In fact, it is frequently easier for an employed person to find a well-paid employment outlet than for one who is unemployed. Managements are prone to assume that employees who have had to be laid off are likely to be the least satisfactory. Whether the dismissal of certain workers has been because of their wage-rates having been forced up through strike-threat coercion, or because demands for the outputs into which their inputs are incorporated have fallen, the first to be discharged are not irrationally presumed by other entrepreneurs to be those whose services are judged to be least valuable.

Chapter IV

Pseudo-Idleness in Labor

1
As skill once acquired is seldom lost, pseudo-idleness in labor due to feared loss of specialized skill is rare

"Pseudo-idleness" in labor is important. But its manifestation differs from that in other resources because it arises very seldom from the existence of *specialized skill.* Moreover, it is not easy to apply the criterion which is so clear in the case of equipment, namely, that the capital value of the workers shall be greater than their positive net scrap value, while their immediate net hire value is nil. There is no such thing as the scrapping of a human being's *powers,* and hence no conception analogous to scrap value in respect of skill. The improvement and specialization of a person do not resemble the specialization physically embodied in a machine. They are the result of environment and upbringing in which deliberate training and education are important. What has once been learned may often be remembered for life. An individual's specialization may be *unutilized* and may deteriorate (as a machine may depreciate) but it is never purposely destroyed. For most types of skill, there is no reason to suppose that work in another job will cause the loss of skill or loss of adaptation to the main occupation faster than idleness. Nor can it often be necessary to destroy one skill in order to supplant another. In general, the skilled worker whose services aré dispensed with is free to employ his acquired talents again, if circumstances should be once more propitious. Thus, when an unemployed linotype operator becomes a shop assistant, it is evidence of a much smaller loss of capital than is indicated when a linotype machine is completely scrapped and the steel turned into shop fittings. We cannot say that the specialization of a linotype operator is as good as "scrapped" because his wage rate in that trade has fallen below what he can earn as a shop assistant (without special training). He leaves the printing works for the counter; but if it is expected that the demand for printing will revive, there is nothing in his temporary shop employment which will prevent his specialization being utilized later on. Labor is, therefore, usually in a very different position from plant and equipment.

2
The destruction of skill

But although rare, the acquisition of a new skill *does* sometimes happen to weaken one which already exists. To take an extreme case, displaced musicians employed on roadmaking may have subtlety of touch destroyed. Where such loss of specialization is important, "pseudo-idleness" may arise through it. The individual may refuse available temporary work because to accept it will cause him to lose skill or his adaptation to the tasks of his main profession faster than physical idleness. His condition ought, therefore, to be thought of as "pseudo-idleness." He is paid for the condition, although his remuneration for the service of preserving his specialization from destruction is postponed until an opening for his special powers *has* been found in the labor market.

3

Important cases of pseudo-idleness arise when supplementary employments will destroy simple availability for more profitable employments

There is, however, a very important form in which "pseudo-idleness" in labor occurs. Its presence may sometimes be manifested in the "casual labor" condition, and it will be best if we consider it in connection with that problem. The essence of the idleness is again availability, in spite of specialized powers as usually understood not being a factor in the situation. "Labor reserves" exist because those forming them have no *immediate hire value,* this last phrase being interpreted in a rather special sense. The acceptance of supplementary employment will cause a more than countervailing decline in long-run expectations of earnings through the loss of availability for relatively more profitable employments. *Availability* is, as we have said, a form of specialization.

4

Workers in pseudo-idleness are paid to keep themselves attached to a trade

To consider the "reserve of labor" (as it has been called) * which tends to become attached to certain occupations, let us for the moment ignore the possibilities: (*a*) of the labor reserve being the product of a wage rate fixed at above the true market rate; and (*b*) of casual work being preferred (in any sense) to regular employment by those engaged in it. If the reserve then exists, the idle workers are, in fact, paid to keep themselves attached to the trade. To the extent that any trade is known to be risky from the point of view of continuity of employment, so must an increment to compensate the workers for such idleness as is liable to be experienced be reckoned as forming part of the remuneration. This has been a commonplace of labor theory at least since the time of Adam Smith. But its significance requires further discussion.

5

The payment for pseudo-idleness in labor is not
a retaining fee, but favorable "expectation of earnings"

*   To think realistically of a "reserve" of labor attached to any occupation, we must envisage this service of *availability*. In the case of a true labor "reserve" it is advantageous to pay for it during actual employment through the ruling wage rates. The irksomeness and cost of attracting labor from temporary occupations when it is wanted makes some payment for continuous availability economical. Under casual labor the increment is received by the workers, not in the form of a *retaining fee* as compensation for the value of their chance of temporary earnings elsewhere, but through the net estimated advantageousness to them of being attached to the occupation being more than they could command in other occupations.[1] The equilibrium is

---

[1] Adam Smith brought in an additional suggestion to explain an element in the remuneration of casual employment. "What he earns," wrote Smith, "while he is employed, must not only maintain him while he is idle, *but make him some compensation for those anxious and desponding moments which the thought of so precarious a situation must sometimes occasion.*" (*Wealth of Nations,* Cannan Edition, vol. I, p. 105. Our italics.) This is obviously an important factor determining the "net advantageousness"

determined by equality of "expectation of earnings," which may be defined as the "wage rate multiplied by the chance of employment." From the workers' point of view, they remain "attached to" the casual trade (and in the extreme case refuse other casual work) because *immediate* availability at all times is a condition of their employment in their principal trade, owing to the *methods of recruitment* believed to be most economical in practice.

6

If "floating labor," unattached to a
particular trade, is a necessary consequence of
productive technique, it is in pseudo-idleness and
remunerated through "expectation of earnings"

"Labor reserves" based on such availability are of even greater importance, however, than the last paragraph would suggest. There are *general* as well as *special* (i.e., attached to particular trades) reserves. Exactly the same considerations apply to those who are "out of work" owing to what are usually called the "inevitable delays" met with in changing from one job to another; the class who, when idle, are not specially attached to any trade at all. The workers affected may be induced not to hide themselves in inferior occupations which might prevent them from being available for more valuable employments which the chance workings of a dynamic society will disclose sooner or later.

---

among those with a certain psychology and tradition. But among the poorest classes, the anxieties are probably more than countervailed by the "benefits" of recurrent "leisure" of the type discussed in Chap. V, paras. 6 and 7. If Adam Smith's classical assertion concerning the influence of the risk burden does happen to be true of this class also, it does not in any way invalidate the analysis in the text.

And the element which remunerates them for this is the extra value of their services in the employments which they expect to find. Perhaps the best example of the situation is that of the "floating labor" in the prewar United States which was unattached to any particular job. This could conceivably have been regarded as falling in part into the "pseudo-idleness" category. The quantity of such idleness is likely to be least, in any given set of technical institutions, where competition can be most effectively secured. As Sir Sydney Chapman wrote in 1908, ". . . to augment the quantity of displacement (of labor) is not to augment the quantity of lengthy unemployment, for the very forces which create the additional displacements induce the reabsorption of the labor displaced. And it is hardly likely that more competition will bring about a better disposition of the old percentage of the population normally employed without increasing it."[2] But in so far as "floating labor" is a necessary consequence of modern technique it is a definitely productive condition and subject to remuneration. The "reserve" represents that disposition of resources which, *given any set of labor market institutions,* is the most productive employment. And for this reason the accompanying "reserve" must be regarded as a case of "pseudo-idleness."

7

*The reality of remuneration
for pseudo-idleness may be simply demonstrated*

To suggest that these "inevitable delays" are "paid for" may at first seem most unrealistic; and a careless reader may well be indignant at such a suggestion. But its truth may be

---

[2] BRASSEY and CHAPMAN, *Work and Wages,* vol. II, p. 349.

simply demonstrated. Improved institutions which reduced the delays of labor transference (commercially run employment exchanges, for instance) would undoubtedly cheapen labor. That is, the amount of productive effort obtainable from a given expenditure on wages would be greater. The saving achieved would represent an economy on the former payment for the availability (not the use in other senses) of a greater quantity. Reserves of labor in certain fields, or completely generalized reserves would be economized. The average period of actual employment for each worker would be longer; and in the light of the principle of equality of expectation of earnings, wage rates would not have to be so high in order to attract a given number of actual workers to any trade which needed their efforts.

8
The typical poverty of
casual workers does not affect the issue

Misconceptions are, however, still likely to arouse indignation when the reader considers the casual labor question, for the workers concerned may in this case be desperately poor. But the fact that their average earnings in casual employment are often pitifully low must not be allowed to distort our judgment on this point.[3] The poverty typical of such workers is due to other causes. Casual labor simply happens to have been the haven into which those debarred or ousted from other trades by labor monopoly have found a permanent or temporary refuge. In spite of its containing only the dregs of employment opportunities, it has pro-

---

[3] No one objects to casual work in a well-paid occupation like, say, that of barristers.

vided the sole considerable palliative to social injustice. Immigrant workers from countries in which opportunities of employment are still less favorable may nevertheless have their inertia overcome by the relatively high earnings obtainable even in the worst labor markets of more favorably situated countries; and their competition may further depress rates of earnings of unskilled and casual labor. In books on the unemployment of labor there seems to have been a curious and perhaps significant reluctance even to mention, let alone bring into discussion, this very crucial fact. But occasionally it *has* been remarked upon. Thus, the Charity Organization Society Committee on Unskilled Labor pointed out in 1908 that "the skilled unions have limited the labor market in their trade. The inevitable result has been to maintain a continual glut in the low-skilled labor market."[4] It is usually held, however, that there is an obvious injustice in the casual labor system.

9
"Labor reserves" are purchased through wage-rates, and cannot be "forced" unless employers' monopoly can destroy labor mobility

*   Yet, "the requirement in each trade of reserves of labor to meet the fluctuations incidental even to years of prosperity"[5] is often regarded as an evil in itself. Some of the discussions of this question have even written in tones which imply that instead of being *paid* to be thus available, the workers are *forced* by "the employers" into a soul-destroying, cruel and wasteful idleness. But unless that sec-

---

[4] Quoted in ALDEN and HAYWARD, *The Unemployable and the Unemployed*, p. 78.

[5] BEVERIDGE, *Unemployment*, p. 13.

tion of capitalists which benefits from the maintenance of "reserves" has some means other than payment of preventing the workers attached to the trade from obtaining alternative employment, we cannot see how it could be. No one has ever argued, as far as we know, that such a power has existed or been exploited.[6] The "reserves" of labor under casual employment are, in fact, paid for and to the interest of those workers who form them. The labor supplied is often necessarily cheap labor; and that being so, it may often pay to employ it extensively rather than intensively. But if the standards of living which earnings can command from this field are deplorably low, it is the causes of the cheapness of the labor and not the methods by which it pays to utilize it which must be blamed. And the labor is cheap because other opportunities of employment are barred to those who provide it.

---

[6] J. S. POYNTZ says (in *Seasonal Trades*, edited by Webb and Freeman, p. 60): "There are many trades where the employer undoubtedly finds it to his advantage to keep a large fringe of superfluous labor attached to his business in case of extra demand." But as this phenomenon is supposed to be specially prominent in the "sweated industries" where "employers" are notoriously uncombined, the allegation is obviously misconceived. "The army of men and women standing at (the employers') beck and call," says the same writer, "cost him nothing except for the actual hours that they are at work" (ibid., p. 7). This sort of confusion has probably been responsible for an immense amount of avoidable poverty.

Appendix

Notes and Comments on Chapter IV

W hat we describe in paragraph 4 as "the true market   4
rate" of wages can be more appropriately termed "the
market-clearing rate." We have elsewhere[1] defined "market-
clearing prices" *for inputs* as those prices "which induce
investment in all inputs which lack more remunerative fields
of utilization, because prospective yields to the entrepreneurial intermediary from increments acquired exceed or do
not fall short of the market rate of interest."

The type of *pseudo*-idleness in labor discussed in paragraphs 4 and 5 can be further illustrated by the case of   4, 5
attorneys, architects and consultants generally, particularly
in their early years of practice. The sporadic use of their
skills makes essential the prospect of fees high enough to
remunerate their availability. It is through such prospects
that they are induced to choose and train for professions of
spasmodic demand.

Paragraphs 8 and 9 illustrate the socially ameliorative   8, 9

---

[1] HUTT, *Say's Law,* p. 20.

and nonexploitative nature of the relatively low wage-rates which make it profitable to offer sub-optimal employments. These employments mitigate the lot of the many workers who, through the strike-threat system or licensing systems (which allow the more productive occupations to be engrossed for privileged workers), are condemned to work of relatively low value. The interpretation of experience in this case is made difficult when immigrant labor is permitted and profitable to the immigrant, for it further reduces the wage-rates at which predicted marginal yields to entrepreneurs do not fall short of forecast input costs.

But the word "glut," in the passage quoted from a Charity Organization Society Committee Report by Alden and Hayward, is quite inappropriate even when (for reasons to be discussed later) there is unemployment among unskilled workers or those performing mere "put-and-carry" tasks. Immigrants from poor countries often regard as a powerful attraction those wage-rates at which the unemployed in affluent countries would indignantly prefer idleness. We return to this topic in the appendix to Chapter V. On the notion of "glut," see Chapter XII, paragraph 2.

Chapter V

Preferred Idleness

1
Preferred idleness is found in labor only. The simplest case is preference for leisure

The cases which fall under the heading "preferred idleness" are unique because they apply realistically to labor only. There are no important parallels to be distinguished in respect of capital equipment;[1] and with natural resources, the only realistic parallel is that of parks and estates, which are better thought of as utilized. The most obvious actual case is leisure, the preferred alternative to earned money income. Holidays are *in part* to be regarded as leisure. Nonworking hours may *usually* be rightly thought of as leisure (although a genuine yearning for leisure has seldom been a powerful factor in agitations for collective or enforced reductions of the working day).[2]

*

---

[1] The consumption of leisure on the part of the workers, and the necessity of rest and sleep for them, become expressed in social habits and institutions. Indirectly, therefore, these things certainly contribute to the idleness of tools and plant during nonworking hours. The multiple shift device could conceivably be widely adopted, however, without necessitating any sacrifice of leisure on the workers' part.

[2] See HUTT, *Economists and the Public,* pp. 176–77, 279–80.

2

Things like pride, prestige, boredom
or laziness may lead to idleness being preferred
to the return from employment

*   But there are other kinds of idleness which, while they
might not be understood as leisure in ordinary parlance,
partake of its nature and are accurately described as "preferred" idleness. Consider the person who refuses available
work because it is *infra dig.* The acceptance of a much
lower salary may so wound the pride of a displaced middle-
class employee that he will for long fritter away his own
savings or the earnings of his family and friends, and
endure relative penury, rather than admit to himself (or the
circle that knows him) the loss of income status to which he
has been subjected. A similar case is that in which it is
the nature of available work itself, more than the salary
which it commands, which makes idleness the preferred
alternative. The poor whites in South Africa have been
most reluctant to take on "Kaffir work," even when it has
been offered by the State at subsidized rates more than
double those paid to the despised natives. Moreover, there
are sets of people whose social environment and sources of
income are such that they are not impelled to spend much
of their time or any of their time in remunerative employment. Work for which they are qualified may seem to be so
irksome or boring that they will do almost anything to
avoid it. The disutility of such work, as some economists
prefer to say, may be high. Especially will this be so if
custom or public opinion in any social class condones, or
does not condemn "laziness," "sponging" or "parasitism."
It has long been recognized that with many primitive races

brought suddenly into the industrial system, the supply of labor in terms of hours of work offered will be more likely to fall than rise if their rates of earnings are increased. And the same phenomenon is occasionally experienced under the industrial system. As Professor Pigou has put it, "the effort demand of workers for stuff is inelastic"[3] in conceivable situations. Larger earnings will mean that more leisure will be purchased.

3
The preference for idleness may depend upon attachment to a district where an individual has relatives or friends and a customary mode of living

One of the circumstances in which these considerations are of importance is in respect of the geographical incidence of unemployment. The so-called immobility of labor, the inertia which prevents "labor transference," is due largely to the individual's fondness for a district in which he has long resided, perhaps the district of his birth. If he leaves a "distressed area," say, he must bid good-bye to his friends and sometimes forsake his customary mode of living. Certainly his "lack of initiative" may be deplored on the grounds that it is against his "true interests"; but given the absence of social inducements to migrate (e.g., sufficiently attractive wage-rates in other parts) or the absence of social coercions enforcing migration,[4] his unemployment must be regarded as the fulfillment of his preferences.

---

[3] PIGOU, *Theory of Unemployment*, p. 6.

[4] Social coercions enforcing migration will be effective if there is no unemployment insurance or other local source of income. However, a case can be made for unemployment insurance to facilitate the process of prospecting for an employment outlet.

4

Given the social will, preferred idleness
implies no wrong use of resources but might
be deplorable on moral grounds

In modern societies we usually regard a high demand for leisure in the senses just discussed (when it occurs among those condemned to a relatively low standard of material living) as evidence of demoralization. In extreme cases, those in the poorer classes who express such preferences are classed as "won't works," described as "work shy" and so forth; and they are thought of as a social problem. Now the cause of unemployment in this case is a preference. It implies no wrong use of resources, given the social will. If it is a condition which we happen to deplore on *moral* grounds, then the method of reform lies either in changing the preferences directly (through preaching or teaching) or in changing the environment which apparently gives rise to the despised preferences.

5

Preferred idleness among the "work shy" tends to
vary according to the income available without work

The preference of the "work shy" for idleness is almost certainly subject to the law that the smaller the individual's savings, or the smaller the available assistance of his relatives, his friends, an insurance fund, or the State, the less likely will he be to demand it. The *importance* of this empirical law (which might well be reversed under different traditions from those which exist today) is rather indefinite: the *fact* of its existence is indisputable.[5] There have always been

---

[5] There are cases which are difficult to interpret. Thus, if a wife leaves the

men who have frankly said: "I don't feel any obligation to work as long as I can live by other means."[6] And there have been authorities who have regarded such an attitude as being so common among large groups of people as to constitute a major cause of idleness in labor.[7] Thus, the Departmental Committee on Vagrancy reported in 1906 that "were it not for the indiscriminate dole-giving which prevails—idle vagrancy, ceasing to be a profitable profession, would come to an end."[8] What will not be denied is that, as things are today, the availability of an income without work acts as a stimulus to "preferred idleness." And if we believe that this is to be deplored, we can devise appropriate reforms. Edu-

---

wage-paid labor market when her husband succeeds in earning more, it may be to devote more time to the adequate performance of household services. If so, it would be most realistic to regard her condition not as "preferred idleness" of the leisure variety but as employed, she having exercised a new preference not involving idleness in any sense. More domestic services are purchased at the cost of the wife's money income foregone. If she seeks household work because she enjoys it, we may or may not find it convenient to think of her work as a leisure occupation like, for example, the hard day's work which an amateur gardener puts in. But if we *do* call it "idleness" or "unemployment" we must recognize it as a "preferred" condition. The refusal of wage-paid labor by the "unemployed" worker who possesses an allotment which brings him some income in kind is a similar case. If we think it realistic to describe his state as "idle," then we must regard it as "preferred idleness." It is not necessarily a condition to be deplored.

[6] See ALDEN and HAYWARD, *The Unemployable and the Unemployed,* p. 46.

[7] There have been penalties for vagrancy in England at all times, ancient, medieval and modern. This suggests that there must have been a taste for it. It suggests also that physical existence has been fairly easily maintained in respect of food and clothing by those who survived childhood. For in spite of the occurrence of periodic starvation until the industrial revolution was firmly established, the loss of large numbers in that way was always regarded as a catastrophe.

[8] Quoted in ALDEN and HAYWARD, op. cit., p. 26.

cation, the creation of an ambition-awakening tradition, the stimulation of public contempt for the individual who draws from the pool without contributing to it, the cutting down of unconditional help[9]—all these may prove to be remedial policies. But as philosophers we must keep quite separate in our minds the traditional and environmental factors[10] which seem to give rise to demoralizing preferences like laziness, and *the fact* of those preferences.

6

Preferred idleness may arise through
a preference for jobs giving intermittent leisure

Having dealt with the nature of preferred idleness, we can consider a more complex form, namely, that which is spasmodic, recurrent. This is a factor contributing to the "net advantageousness" of "casual labor" from the worker's point of view. The intermittent leisure may be an end for which a sacrifice will be made. Nearly a century ago, the connection between the irksomeness of regular laboring work and the existence of vagrancy and casual labor was

---

[9] "Preferred idleness" of the type which might be deplored is probably least where the funds on which the individual lives are provided by himself, his family or his friends. His family and friends will prevent what they would regard as abuse of their support. There has so far been no "unemployment problem" in the popular sense among the urban natives in South Africa partly, it seems, because, having been political and social pariahs, no system of organized relief has been devised for their unemployed. They are maintained by their friends who know them. But it must be remembered also that the absence of tacit or formal labor organization and the absence of wage fixation in the fields of employment in which they are permitted to compete, results in "enforced idleness" or "withheld capacity" being absent among them as well.

[10] E.g., the ineffectiveness of current moral instruction, or what we may hold to be distributive and other injustices.

noticed by Senior who said: "We believe, after all, that nothing is so much disliked as steady, regular labor; and that the opportunities of idleness afforded by an occupation of irregular employment are so much more than an equivalent for its anxiety, as to reduce (such wages) . . . below the common average."[11] This assertion has obviously much less truth in Great Britain today than it had at earlier times; but in 1911 Messrs. Rowntree and Lasker commented on the same fact. They regarded it not as the manifestation of an inherent preference but as in itself a result of irregularity. They remarked of some youths whose first employment was as casual laborers: "Frequently they play about in the streets for so long that when they actually begin work they resent discipline, and will throw up a job on the slightest provocation. Many of them soon learn to prefer an easy life as casual 'hands' with considerable intervals of loafing at street corners, to regular work."[12]

7

If cases of preferred idleness are held to be "demoralizing," decasualization might be a remedy

If it is true that "preferred" idleness of this kind is the product of a demoralization which that idleness itself creates; if the psychological effect of an irregular income is to create a degrading dislike for continuous work;[13] if, in

---

[11] *Political Economy*, 4th edition, 1858, p. 208. Adam Smith stressed only the anxiety aspect which, he thought, tended to make average earnings in casual occupations above, not below the average. See Chap. IV, para. 5 (footnote).

[12] ROWNTREE and LASKER, *Unemployment*, 1911, p. 6.

[13] It is very common to argue that "irregularity of income is a much more important source of pauperism than low wages" (FELDMAN, *The Regularization of Employment*, p. 24). But the ultimate verdict of sociologists

other words, the taste for casual labor is a bad taste, and also self-perpetuating, a case for decasualization can be made out. But so far as youths are concerned, a more effective remedy seems to be compulsory education during the intervals of idleness. And compulsory decasualization for adults has many dangers. Indeed, the justification for such a restraint of preferences must rest upon grounds which, as far as the author's knowledge goes, have never been appealed to on this topic in the whole literature relevant to the question, namely, the grounds justifying the *educative restraint* of adults.[14] And the arguments for such restraint must be viewed in the light of considerations relative to "pseudo-idleness" and "labor reserves" (which we have already discussed in Chapter IV, paragraphs 3 to 9) and "participating idleness" (which we shall discuss in Chapter VIII, paragraphs 8 to 10). All three conceptions: "pseudo-idleness," "preferred idleness" and "participating idleness" must complicate realistic study of the casual labor problem. The enforcement of such decasualization might be achieved by the removal of the alternatives which militate against continuous work. Thus, to the extent to which this form of "preferred idleness" is due to the conditions noticed in paragraph 5 (namely, knowledge that relief to prevent actual physical suffering will almost certainly be available when required), the administration of relief with greater strin-

---

will probably be that the source of demoralization is the lack of hope and the absence of outlets for the achievement of any form of distinction and social respect. The physical side of poverty has been greatly overstressed because the propagandist has found it easier to win support by emphasizing that side than by arguing the superficially less plausible case against environmental factors which are not in such concrete evidence.

[14] See HUTT, *Economists and the Public,* Chap. XVII, on "Educative Restraints of Freedom of Choice."

gency will supply the coercion for an increased measure of "desirable" decasualization.

8
The "reckless" and "lazy" casual laborer
in preferred idleness may simply be relying upon
the fact that he will not be allowed to starve

Whether we are justified in regarding the taste which   *
demands "preferred" idleness in these circumstances as a deplorable taste, or as the expression of a wholly regrettable irrationality, is by no means clear. The fact that such poor appear to "live for the moment," to have no foresight, to be extravagant with their earnings which "come in spurts," and to be willing to rely upon relief when they have no money, may simply show that, even in their poverty, the physical side of existence means less to them than other things. They want the excitement which can be purchased by the pathetic "extravagances" in which they are led to indulge when they have the means. The social philosopher who accepts the liberal ideal has some reasons for seeing in preferences of this kind a longing for "higher and better things." In spite of the condemnation of thriftlessness by the conventional moralists, the "fatalism," the "absence of worry," the apparent recklessness and the laziness of the poor may be viewed as their very realistic appreciation of the fact that they will not be allowed to starve. If that is so, who can blame them? Are the individual mental adjustments which lead to such traditions so very foolish? After all, are not the poorest classes condemned, under our present social arrangements, to permanently low incomes?

Appendix

Notes and Comments on Chapter V

Our contention in paragraph 1 that the simplest case of "preferred idleness" is leisure may be misleading without some qualification. Such idleness arises, of course, when the marginal value of leisure to a worker exceeds all wage-rate offers known to him. Thus, the concept can be considered ethically neutral. We see no reason at all why any person should not feel morally free to purchase leisure through the sacrifice of material income, as long as it is not at the expense of his children or other dependents. But if he *does* purchase leisure to the extent that he is impoverished, that must necessarily affect the ethical aspect of any claim on his part for support from the taxpayer or the charitable. Has he a claim similar to that of the crippled, the deaf, or the blind?

The reference in paragraph 2 to the "poor Whites" of South Africa is now rather dated. In the 1930s, they constituted a problem of major urgency. Today that is no longer true.

The word "Natives" for "Blacks" has been wisely abandoned in South Africa. "Africans" has been difficult to use because of a clash with the long-accepted name for the majority of the whites, "Afrikaners," whose home language is "Afrikaans." Besides, the Whites of the Republic of South Africa and of Rhodesia also regard themselves as "Africans."

8   The reference in paragraph 8 to "the poorest classes condemned, under our present social arrangements, to permanently low incomes," ought, we now feel, to have mentioned the principal causes of impoverishment, namely, (a) governmental tolerance of strike-threat pressures,[1] (b) government-enacted minimum wage-rates, (c) income transfers which cause the squandering of part of the stock of assets (especially of those which tend most effectively to multiply the yield to human effort), and (d) prolonged, compulsory, unproductive schooling, of which the true intention is to keep juveniles off the labor market for as long as possible.[2]

In spite of insistence in this chapter that the term "preferred" has a nonemotive connotation, some critics have suggested that it is an adjective which inevitably evokes disapproval. We maintain, however, that any stigma attaching

---

[1] See HUTT, *Strike-Threat; Collective Bargaining.*

[2] When such schooling *is* unproductive, it is a form of enforced idleness— perhaps better termed enforced leisure. There is then a sacrifice of the potential product of juvenile labor and hence a loss of an important potential contribution to the source of demands. Moreover, not only does boredom tend to demoralize those young people who are denied the right to contribute to general well-being, but purposeless schooling withholds education by frustrating the possibility of early investment in human capital. The education withheld includes not only the inculcation of technical skills but the imparting of improved literacy and arithmetic both of which it is to the advantage of managements to provide.

to the word must be due to the spontaneous moral judgment of the reader.

Let us consider, for instance, the position of the eight million unemployed in the United States in 1976 (with 20 percent teen-age employment and 30 percent among black teen-agers) in relation to *illegal* immigration. If there were no surveillance on the Mexican border a veritable deluge of Mexicans would result. With great ingenuity, these industrious and enterprising aliens would try to, and often succeed in dodging minimum wage exclusions and accept work on terms that, for them, would mean affluence. And it is not only Mexicans who find highly attractive the prospect of earnings at which poor Americans (of all racial groups) prefer idleness. Illegal immigrants manage to slip into the United States from all parts of the world at an estimated rate of about 800,000 a year.[3] In 1975, 480 were tracked down in Georgia. They had come from 71 countries. In Dallas, there was a similar story. In 1975, an estimated 800,000 of those attempting to enter the United States illegally were turned back at points of entry; about the same number managed to get through; and about the same number, who had previously entered illegally, were at last discovered, and deported.

The fact is that the least well-paid, unfilled employment outlets in the United States offer such improvements in living standards and prospects for so many foreigners that they have enticed in about eight million in all. Prospective earnings which poor Americans would reject cause poor

[3] The figures in this paragraph are all taken from a paper read to the Dallas Council on World Affairs on February 24, 1976, on behalf of L. F. Chapman, Commissioner of the U. S. Immigration and Naturalization Service.

foreigners to leave their loved ones and enter illegally. They often use their meager savings to travel great distances; they are prepared to endure severe hardships and privation during their travels; and they are prepared to commit fraud and forgery at the boundaries and accept the risks of immigration law penalties—all this for the opportunity of selling their efforts in the United States. But the point is that the work they contribute has presumably been refused by huge numbers of unemployed Americans, including juveniles.

The labor offered by these industrious aliens seems to have been absorbed easily, especially in the large metropolitan areas. It must make a really considerable contribution to the source of demands for noncompeting labor and productive services generally.[4] Hence to refer to that part of the eight million domestic unemployed who reject the jobs that the aliens so eagerly seek as in "preferred idleness" can hardly be thought of as a pejorative or dyslogistic use of words.

Again in South Africa, hordes of foreign Africans from all over the continent would flock into that country were there no barriers to immigration.[5] The rising real wage rates of recent years for what remain sub-optimal employments

---

[4] Congressmen financed by the labor unions are prone to complain that many of these immigrants are thrifty and generous. They refrain from consuming the whole value of their outputs, sending a portion of their income back to their families abroad. In so doing, of course, the immigrants do not raise the value of employment outlets at home as much as they would if all their income were used (for consumption *plus* savings) in the United States. Yet foreign travel by nationals is seldom condemned, although it has the same effect and the motive is less praiseworthy.

[5] See Chap. IX, para. 4 and W. H. HUTT, *Economics of the Colour-Bar*, Institute of Economic Affairs, London, 1964.

in the types of work to which the greater (if declining) proportion of black workers in South Africa are still confined would have been achieved very much more slowly had it not been for restraints on black immigration and the temporary migrant influx. But the Blacks of South Africa have been denied effective labor unions so that unemployment among them has been a very minor problem.

Addendum

Some Recent Discussions of "Preferred Idleness"

The "preferred idleness" aspect of joblessness, without the use of this realistic term, has been treated well in the three recent discussions of "leisure" and "unemployment" referred to in the Preface to this Second Edition (p. 19). The conclusions of the authors there mentioned on this subject are remarkably similar to ours, although those authors were obviously unaware of our 1939 contribution. However, on what many readers may regard as a minor point, we feel that Heyne and Johnson's outstanding textbook may mislead. They treat an increased demand for leisure as "less *time* supplied to the labor market" (our italics).[1] Admittedly, most work supplied is remunerated according to time and not "by piece"—i.e., not by measured product. But the price of any additional leisure acquired is surely most usefully envisaged in terms of a reduced value of inputs supplied to the productive process. Actually, Heyne and Johnson themselves come near to stating things just this way when they

---

[1] PAUL HEYNE and THOMAS JOHNSON, *Toward Economic Understanding,* Science Research Associates, Palo Alto, Ca., 1976, p. 420.

point out that leisure is demanded by those who place "a marginal value on leisure that is *greater* than the available wage rate," i.e., a value which exceeds the value to others of their contributions to the flow of income.[2]

The contributions to which we now refer, however, bring out *inter alia,* illustrated by practical examples, a crucial point we made earlier about the several different "causes" of idleness which have to be distinguished. Each of these causes is often, if not normally, combined with other "causes" to produce one superficially homogenous condition—"idleness."

Perceiving this, Feldstein, and Heyne and Johnson, are led to a conclusion which they state more strikingly than we did in 1939. Following an empirical approach, Feldstein states it in an italicized passage: *"The current structure of unemployment in the American economy is not compatible with the traditional view of hard core unemployed who are unable to find jobs."*[3] And in respect of teenage employment he concludes that "among the young and single . . . high wages encourage an increased demand for leisure."[4] "Many young persons want more leisure than is consistent with full-time employment." He adds that such remarks "are not to be intended as criticism,"[5] and he compares, very effectively, preferred idleness among juveniles in the labor market with the leisure enjoyed by students. "The extremely high unem-

---

[2] In other words, the marginal pecuniary value of the services that people provide as inputs exceeds the marginal value to them of additional increments of leisure.

[3] MARTIN FELDSTEIN, "The Economics of the New Unemployment," *The Public Interest,* Fall 1973, p. 9.

[4] Ibid., p. 11.

[5] Ibid., p. 13.

ployment rates are therefore not quite what they seem. They reflect . . . the temporary and voluntary unemployment that young people can afford in an affluent society." This gives rise, he says, to "a real and serious problem."[6] He blames in part "the unsatisfactory type of job that is available to many young workers . . . often dead-end jobs with neither opportunity for advancement within the firm nor training and experience that would be useful elsewhere."[7]

Such employment outlets are, however, almost wholly such as we have classified under the "sub-optimal" category. They should properly be seen as society's method of mitigating the impoverishing consequences of the strike-threat system.

On this issue we feel that Feldstein has not fully shown the extent to which any increase in employment (i.e., any addition to inputs) tends to raise the purchasing power offered in noncompeting employment outlets. He explains that "it is clear that there is no lack of jobs in the sense that nearly any young person can get a job," but he is "not certain that *all* could."[8] In the light of Say's law, however, whenever any young person *does* take a job, *ceteris paribus,* the easier it will be for *others* to get a job[9] (although not necessarily of course in the same occupation, firm or industry).

Heyne and Johnson write, "People are always unemployed by choice,"[10] i.e., not by necessity. Under "choice" of "leisure," however, they include *job search*—prospecting

---

[6] Ibid., p. 14.

[7] Ibid., p. 14.

[8] Ibid., p. 15.

[9] See in particular, our *Say's Law.*

[10] HEYNE and JOHNSON, op. cit., p. 432.

for more productive and hence better remunerated employment—whereas we insist that, *in itself,* the process is neither unemployment nor choice of leisure. Yet they themselves, following their immediate inspirers, Feldstein, and Alchian and Allen (and the ultimate inspirer, Hayek),[11] stress again and again that job search *activities* are a vital part of the general market function of acquiring necessary and costly information, and that this is obviously a productive kind of employment. That is why, in 1939, we compared the process to "prospecting," searching for knowledge of employment outlets. Such job searchers are entrepreneurs, *choosing means to ends.* Hence we must conceive of their decision-making as expressing a "judgment" as distinct from a "preference," the latter meaning a *choice of ends.* It is our considered opinion that this distinction assists conceptual clarity. And we feel that the process is productive employment rather than "a productive way in which to use leisure," as Heyne and Johnson describe it.[12]

But we are not denying that this important form of employment may be pursued in a leisurely way. Indeed we have emphasized that unemployment compensation *may* subsidize job search activities; and because a subsidy must, in some measure, cause such activities to rise on the scales of preference of the officially "unemployed," the numbers so engaged may be expected to grow. There may well be, therefore, an important *element* of preferred idleness among those searching for employment outlets. And in extreme cases

---

[11] F. A. HAYEK, "The Use of Knowledge in Society," American Economic Review, 1945, reprinted by Institute for Humane Studies, Menlo Park, Ca., 1971; "Full Employment at Any Price," Institute of Economic Affairs, London, 1975.

[12] HEYNE and JOHNSON, op. cit., p. 421.

the job search aspect could be little more than pretense, actual unemployment being purely "preferred." On the other hand, because one man's return to directly remunerated work tends to raise demands for another person's services, such a subsidy *could* be productive.

Another aspect of preferred idleness in labor which we did not fully consider in our 1939 treatment concerns *average periods of unemployment*. Such averages are obviously relevant to people's valuations of pecuniary or material income in relation to the benefits of "freedom from work" (leisure preference). They differ considerably from country to country, region to region, industry to industry, occupation to occupation, race to race,[13] as between men and women and as between different age groups. But in every case the average period for which a person officially classified as unemployed is idle is almost certainly much smaller than most writers on the subject appear to perceive.

Feldstein's empirical studies have shown that, in the United States (where the proportion of unemployed to the total work force is much greater than it is in deeply depressed Britain), "almost everyone who is out of work can find his usual type of job in a relatively short time."[14] But because so many of the available jobs are "unattractive," they are not accepted. He draws attention to the relevant statistics.[15] During the heavy unemployment of 1971, which

---

[13] Feldstein points out that in the United States, "non-white unemployment rates are higher in every category," and that "unemployment due to voluntary separations and withdrawals from the labor force is approximately twice the level for whites." FELDSTEIN, op. cit., p. 9.

[14] Ibid., p. 5.

[15] See also A. A. ALCHIAN and W. R. ALLEN, *University Economics*, Wadsworth Publishing Co., Belmont, Ca., 1972, pp. 518–19.

created so much concern, "45 percent of the unemployed had been out of work for less than five weeks." In 1969, only 10.4 percent of all the unemployed had been out of work for more than twenty-seven weeks, and more than half of the unemployed had voluntarily quit (not been laid off from) their previous jobs. Further, in the unskilled and juvenile labor fields, voluntary job leaving is encouraged "since comparable jobs are easy to find,"[16] and also because the relatively high wage-levels for those entering the labor market "encourage an increased demand for leisure."[17] These are among the reasons why job leavers contributed in 1971 "more than two-thirds of the unemployment among teenaged, experienced workers."[18] It is equally important to notice that job loss "accounts for less than half of total unemployment."[19] Hence, the very high unemployment rate in the United States, especially among juveniles, reflects "the temporary and voluntary unemployment that young people can afford in an affluent society."[20]

At no time does Feldstein suggest that those who accept such forms of preferred idleness are blameworthy. The disincentive to work is due not only to the general affluence which eases the lot of the unemployed, but the "unattractiveness" of available work and the absence of sufficient prospects of training for advancement.

This last-mentioned consideration may possibly be of great importance. There are powerful entrepreneurial incentives to invest in human capital through the inculcation

---

[16] FELDSTEIN, op. cit., p. 11.

[17] Ibid., p. 11.

[18] Ibid., p. 12.

[19] Ibid., p. 6.

[20] Ibid., p. 14.

of skills. But these profit incentives are seriously attenuated because of the minimum wage impact. "A firm can," writes Feldstein, "generally provide the opportunity to acquire new marketable skills," but "only to a worker whose net product *during the period of training* is at least equal to his wage. Unfortunately, the current minimum wage law prevents many young people from accepting" such jobs.[21] For the disadvantaged group to produce "enough to earn the minimum wage is incompatible with the opportunity for adequate on-the-job learning. For this group the minimum wage implies high short-run unemployment and the chronic poverty of a life of low-wage jobs."[22]

But the real psychological barrier which leads juveniles to prefer leisure to the enormous advantages of prospectively valuable training within industry is, in our own judgment, not due solely to today's relatively high free-market value of juvenile earnings and the minimum wage system. It must be blamed even more on the general suppression of prospects of advancement through enforcement of the "rate for the job" via the strike-threat. This is (and, we believe, always has been) the most effective method of restraint of entry to any occupation or industry that has ever been invented. It shuts off access to the bargaining table of all initially less competent and "non-preferred" groups. But what may be even worse, it destroys access to training for those who must otherwise be confined to dull "put and carry" work in sub-optimal occupations. Of what use are acquired skills or special knowledge if those who achieve them have poor prospects of ever being able to use them

---

[21] Ibid., p. 14.
[22] Ibid., pp. 14–15. Compare ALCHIAN and ALLEN, op. cit., pp. 514–15.

with profit? What incentive is there if virtually no hope exists of ever competing against others so qualified?

Feldstein advocates the subsidization of "on-the-job training" as a politically acceptable way of maintaining the workers' earnings while the minimum wage-rate is reduced to compensate. But in a free labor market, would not such a subsidy be superfluous? We suggest that an enormous investment in human capital in the form of job training would become profitable, with a formidable rise in the wages-flow, if fears of private coercion *intended* to exploit investors could be removed.

Between thirty and forty years ago there was almost a crusade for "T.W.I." ("training within industry"), and the purpose was less to create attractive employment openings than to provide prospects of advancement. For this reason we are far from certain that Feldstein's positive and thoughtful proposal could circumvent the true obstacle, which is the closing of so many doors to promotion by the labor unions. As things are, strike-threat enforcement of "the rate for the job" remains, by all odds, the most vicious obstacle. If the constitutional right of every person to free individual access to every wage bargaining table could be effectively assured, together with the concomitant right to bid, without restraint from his competitors, for any employment which he believes will improve his earnings, prospects and conditions of service—in short, if the worker could be emancipated from the closed shop type of detriment (in the United States, if 14b of the Taft-Hartley Act could be enshrined in federal law, *to apply in all states*), it seems certain that the problem would cure itself.[23]

---

[23] Provided of course that the minimum wage-rates were not again raised,

What important practical conclusion is suggested by our analysis of the "preferred idleness" condition? It can be best stated in quotations from the two textbook discussions of unemployment to which we have already referred. The first is from Alchian and Allen, who categorically deny the common assertion that unemployment exists because "there are not enough jobs available." They remark:

> Sometimes it is asserted that there are not enough jobs available. This assertion is simply unacceptable if reality is to be recognized. Jobs are always available, but the wage offer may be unacceptably low in view of alternative prospects or leisure.[24]

The importance of rigorous, dispassionate thinking about the truth which the above passage brings out can scarcely be exaggerated. In the second quotation, Heyne and Johnson further illustrate the point at issue:

> People were *looking* for work in 1944 not because they couldn't find employment, but because they wanted *better* jobs than the ones they already knew about. They were unemployed *by choice* and not involuntarily. And that leads to the somewhat controversial proposal that we shall now offer and defend: People are always unemployed by choice.[25]

---

which would sabotage the required incentive. It would simply reimpose that protection of the relatively rich at the expense of the relatively poor which has now become traditional.

[24] ALCHIAN and ALLEN, op. cit., p. 515.

[25] HEYNE and JOHNSON, op. cit., p. 432.

Chapter VI

Irrational Preferred Idleness[1]

1

*Consumers are apt to be more vigilant
in respect of the price than the quality of a commodity*

At this stage, we must consider a very important element
in those preferences whose fulfillment is found in idleness. All human tastes seem to be fashioned in part by
contact with irrational influences. Wicksteed, in particular,
has drawn our attention to this. If the price of a thing falls,
we are apt to buy more of it simply because it is "so cheap,"
irrespective of whether at its reduced value that new distribution of expenditure most effectively contributes to (what
must be irrelevant in any purely economic study) the economy of our "private world." If we have been saving to
provide for the future, our strivings are apt to become
embodied in habit, and we may develop miserly traits
which the philosopher might have grounds for saying are
contrary to our "real interests." Moreover, we seem usually

---

[1] The term "irrational preferred idleness" needs some explanation. A *taste*
as such can hardly be "irrational"; but that term can be applied to a *choice*
or *preference* because it may be based upon a false expectation due to its
consequences having been wrongly thought out.

to be much more vigilant in respect of the *price* of a thing that we buy than we are in respect of its *quality*. Unannounced reduction of quality is a frequent response of producers (under imperfect competitive institutions) to a rise in their costs or a fall in their supplementary receipts.[2] They may recognize, rightly, that the substitution to their detriment of consumers' demands is much less likely if there is no obvious and visible rise of price. Whether such policies are morally defensible does not concern the economist. The social philosopher might well defend them if he rejects the consumers' sovereignty ideal. He might regard those moralists who have a fastidious objection to venial deception as troublemakers. And if physical productivity is the philosopher's ideal (not that *we* can suggest any principle of measurement for physical productivity) he may have grounds for deploring policies which cause consumers to be critical of the content of the things their money buys. For ready acquiescence on the consumers' part will bring a greater measure of "orderliness" in the productive system in the sense that inefficient *entrepreneurs* will not suffer losses. Of course, if the deterioration in quality should be suddenly noticed, a difficult situation might arise. But when the goodness of consumers' sovereignty is frankly denied, all difficulties vanish and the "rationalization" or "planning" of consumption can be advocated.

---

[2] The same policy may be followed in other circumstances and with other motives, of course. Thus, under tariff protection plus "rationalization," electric lamp manufacturers may deliberately lower the life of their bulbs with a view to "stimulating consumption," and by so doing bring greater "prosperity" to the industry.

2

*Similarly, workers in general tend to be more
concerned about wage-rates than about the purchasing
power of wages, and in depressions may collectively prefer
unemployment to employment at lower wage-rates*

This apparently irrelevant excursion into the field of
ethics is necessary because similar irrationalities in respect of
reactions to changes in wage-rates may be a factor of some
importance determining the extent of "preferred" idleness;
and in so far as this is so, the same issues of policy arise.
Workers in general are indignant at wage cuts, and their
indignation may become one of the determining factors in
certain of their choices. In practice, their objection as *wage
earners* to downward wage-rate adjustments seems to be
much more serious than their anger *as consumers* at price
increases. How far their attitude is the product of teaching
or propaganda may be a question which the formulators of
policy should consider. But the fact may often be (and it
is alleged by some that in practice this is a matter of great
importance) that many workers will prefer to reject certain
available employment when a wage-rate is cut, while they
will accept that employment in the absence of a cut, although an equal or greater reduction in the rights conferred
by the wage-rate is effected. Concerning those already in
employment, for example, so long as they receive the same
money wage-rate they are relatively satisfied: what are
usually called their "real wages" matter less to them. Perhaps the importance of maintaining the *nominal* wage-rate
lies principally in the fact that the dignity of the worker is
thereby secured.[3] He does not have to confess to reduced

---

[3] A worker's commitments, which are incurred in money, may also make

earning power. Moreover, all other workers are similarly burdened when the price of "wage goods" rises. His line of employment is not *singled out,* so to speak, for a wage cut, to the detriment of his status and self-respect. As some economists prefer to put it, the "disutilities of work" are greater when the nominal wage rate is lower.[4]

3

*Keynes seems to argue that much
idleness is due to irrational preferences which, he
implies, orthodox economists overlooked*

If we have properly understood Keynes' arguments, one of his suggestions is that an important part of what we have called "preferred idleness" is to be attributed to this cause. He calls it "involuntary unemployment" but nevertheless conceives of the condition in terms of willingness to work. One might almost infer that he is trying to distinguish the wage earners' *real* will and their *expressed* will! Orthodox economists, he says, have assumed that all "those who are now unemployed though willing to work at the current wage will withdraw the offer of their labor in the event of even a small rise in the cost of living."[5] It is difficult to

---

it *important* for him that his earnings shall not fall. But this consideration will not lead to "preferred idleness," unless consequent vindictiveness, worry or frustration makes work seem less desirable.

[4] A worker might object for another reason to his line of employment being *singled out* for a wage cut. It might well be that if *all* wage-rates above the competitive were reduced, all workers would be better off; but reductions would, nevertheless, be resisted because no single group of workers could be convinced that the process would be universal, and if it were not widespread the group consenting would be the losers. This is, however, an individually rational but collectively irrational objection to wage cuts, and is a separate point. There is a privately beneficial withholding of capacity. This type of situation is dealt with in Chap. X, paras. 7 to 12.

[5] KEYNES, op. cit., p. 13.

believe that many economists could have been so stupid. They may possibly have misjudged the importance of this type of irrationality. The issue is greatly complicated by the fact that irrationality bears not only upon the determination of "preferred idleness" but also upon that due to what we call "withheld capacity." Restrictionism is not always rational. And, at times, Keynes' "involuntary unemployment" is obviously intended to apply to the results of irrational judgment *in so far as it crystallizes in current restrictive policies.* But his conception of this is never clearly differentiated from the determinants of "preferred idleness" —as we have defined it—which at other times he seems to be considering.[6] Let us at this stage consider the effect upon "preferred idleness." In this case, the orthodox employment theory of the past has in no way been invalidated. Common attempts to apply it may have been misconceived.

4

Although the conception of "irrational preferences" lies outside the province of "pure theory," this has not meant that the economists have been blind to their existence

In "pure theory," the irrational origin of preferences may   * be taken as part of the data in the light of which a particular result may be explained. As soon as we bring the question of "irrationality" into discussion as a phenomenon to be deplored, we have, strictly speaking, left the field of *economic* controversy. In spite of Keynes' adjective "involuntary," the idleness that we are considering is the fulfillment, not the frustration of a preference.[7] If, as econo-

---

[6] This is one of the consequences of the inappropriate simplicity introduced by Keynes to which we have referred in Chap. I, para. 8.

[7] There is, however, an entirely different conception of "involuntary unemployment" in Keynes' book, entangled with the ones we are here dis-

mists, we are asked for its cause, our answer is simple: Well,
they prefer idleness to work at that rate and they take it.
Yet this attitude can be so easily misunderstood and so
easily misrepresented that we must hasten to add that the
economics which gives such a neutral answer to a fiercely
debated question is by no means a useless analysis to the
statesman who is asking how, as a matter of practical policy, "preferred idleness" (deplored on moral grounds) may
be reduced.

5

*The orthodox economists have realistically
recognized the significance of irrational preferences
in relation to scarcity through the conception
of "net advantageousness"*

In practical studies, the economists have always been
realists. Have they not always recognized and accepted as
data (to which their scientific method has been applied)
certain important sources of irrationality? Have they not
frequently stressed the truth that diffused and unseen im-
positions on the individual are acquiesced in and conspicuous burdens objected to? Have they not taken into account
in any practical judgments which they have been called
upon to make the fact that increases of prices of consumers'
goods are often *hardly noticed?* Was this not, indeed, a
central theme of Bastiat's *Ce qu'on voit et ce qu'on ne voit
pas,* which he regarded as *L'Economie Politique en une
Leçon?* And is this not one of the paramount issues which

---

cussing. He seems to hold that if money wage-rates greater than the
competitive are cut, even if universally, it will not lead to the increased
employment which a rise in wage good prices would stimulate. We do not
here attempt to discuss the grounds on which this theory is based.

the serious reformer must always consider? The truth is, of course, that the orthodox economists (when venturing to point out the implications of their science) have been under no illusions as to the existence of pigheadedness, mere pique, feared loss of prestige and dignity, or resentment at "capitalist exploitation," all of which may work to cause wage cuts to be more indignantly viewed than equivalent or greater rises in the prices of "wage goods." They have certainly never built on the assumption which Keynes attributes to them that the supply of labor is "a function of real wages as its sole variable."[8] On the contrary, the classical and orthodox theory of wages has been dominated by the conception of "net advantageousness"; and even if the economists' judgment of the importance of the peculiar elements of disadvantageousness which Keynes stresses has been faulty (and we do not believe that this is so), it gives no shred of justification to his sweeping assertion that, in consequence, "their argument breaks down entirely."[9]

6
It is the statesman rather than the economist who is concerned with the avoidance of the results of irrationality in preferences

The problems that emerge in attempts to consider the "irrational" elements in individual estimates of net advantageousness are not of the kind which economic analysis can solve. The statesman must ask questions of the following kind: Can the results of consumers' or income receivers' irrationality be avoided while the irrationality itself is

---

[8] KEYNES, op. cit., p. 8.
[9] Ibid.

allowed to persist? Is there an *essentially* educative aspect of recommended policies which are otherwise indefensible? Can workers in general be deceived "for their own good" in a manner which will not necessitate further deceptions later on? What sort of authority can really be trusted to deceive workers "for their own good"? Thus, suppose immediately inflationary policies are being considered. The "deception" issue may obviously be relevant, and these further questions also arise: Is an increase of wage good prices justified because it protects the dignity of certain workers whose preference for work is thereby preserved? Can we ignore the corresponding effects upon the claims of creditors who may not be irrational in respect of their contractual income rights? Economic theory can give no answer to these questions. It can throw light upon the nature of inflation, but that is not our present concern.

7
Sources of irrationality unconnected with wage preferences are probably much more serious

*   Moreover, if we are concerned about *one* type of irrationality in the worker's tastes or in his response to the economic complex, surely we ought to consider it in the light of the whole of his tastes and responses, which must be similarly evaluated according to our principles of rationality whatever they may be.[10] If there is some measure of regrettable unemployment due to one cause, must we not envisage this factor in relation to similar causes which operate to the worker's detriment, even if not expressed in "idleness"? Suppose we think (as social reformers) that his

---

[10] I.e., according to our judgment of the individual's long-run real interest.

concern with nominal rather than "real" wage rates is the result of his placing undue importance on his income status; suppose we regard it as a manifestation of an unworthy snobbishness; and suppose we see in it a contributory cause of degrading idleness; can we not pass equally or even more severe strictures on his preferences in respect of many other things? Consider the laborer's expenditure on the cinema, wireless, holidays, sport, gambling and drink. Can we not criticize his wisdom in wrongly estimating consequences in respect of these also? And do we not find in them expressions of irrationality which *most* reformers would admit are of incomparably greater social urgency? Thus, it has been estimated that the average British workman with an income of £2 a week who is not a total abstainer, spends on an average 6s. 6d. on alcohol and 5s. 6d. in net gambling losses; and that a similar workman with £3 a week spends 10s. on alcohol and 8s. in net gambling losses. Hence, if we do venture into the field in which we criticize the wage earner's bad judgment in seeking leisure and spending his income on his own and his family's behalf, should we not ask (in the light of our standards) whether his concern about his income status, or his pigheadedness, or his hatred of his employers and so forth, has an importance anything like the importance of his bad judgment or foolishness in the matter of many other things. In relation to the individual's own "real welfare" and that of his family, is it not clear that his attitude toward his income status (or whatever else happens to be the cause of his indifference to "real" wage-rates) must be a relatively negligible factor? Surely the specific "disutilities" of work discussed in this chapter do not possess the great significance which has been attributed to them. Surely it is doubtful whether "preferred idleness" (as we are regarding it) is so greatly affected by the store which the workers irrationally set on the maintenance of nominal wage-rates. Their resistance to plasticity of wage-rates seems, in fact, to have an entirely different origin to which we have referred briefly in paragraph 3, and which we shall discuss in Chapter X, paragraphs 14 to 16.

Appendix

Notes and Comments on Chapter VI

The nature of the Keynesian fallacy (mentioned in paragraph 4, footnote 7) which, we said, would not be 4 discussed, is now indicated in our appendix to Chapter II. The fundamental error lies in the "unemployment equilibrium" notion, which has been examined in several contributions by the author,[1] who refers to other exposures of the fallacy.

The reference in paragraph 6 to the "obvious relevance" 6 of "the 'deception' issue" to inflationary policies takes for granted, perhaps, that the reader *will* immediately perceive that wholly anticipated inflation is purposeless inflation. But if any Keynesians did perceive that in 1939, they failed (as far as I have been able to trace) to assert this vital principle explicitly or consider its implications. After World War II it began to be mentioned, although the full significance of expectations in this context has only been generally recognized of recent years.

---

[1] "Price Flexibility and Full Employment," in HENRY HAZLITT, ed., *The Critics of Keynesian Economics; Keynesianism,* Chap. IX; *Say's Law.*

7   Our argument at the end of paragraph 7 does not bring out the important truth that the workers' resistance to plasticity of wage-rates is more attributable to irrational *judgments* of long-term advantage than to irrational *preferences*.

Chapter VII

Participating Idleness

1

*Resources are in participating
idleness when their idle existence confers the right
to participate in monopoly revenues*

We come next to the consideration of a condition which can very easily be mistaken, in some circumstances, for "pseudo-idleness." We shall call it "participating idleness."[1] The condition arises when, as the result of a price higher than the competitive, resources remain attached to, or are induced to attach themselves to an occupation in which they are not actually employed. The inducement which prevents their scrapping is the fact that their owners acquire *the privately or legally conferred right of participation in the monopoly revenues* or the chance of so doing. The right is usually contingent upon *some* productive services actually being *offered* in the monopolized field by the participating individual or firm. And some of the services

---

[1] It has been difficult to find a wholly appropriate term for this condition, the adjectives "induced" and "distributive" both having some advantages. But after some deliberation, the term "participating" has seemed most realistic.

available may actually be utilized. But the resources providing those services are either only partially employed or else only intermittently employed. To discuss this question we must make use of the largely self-explanatory conceptions of "enforced idleness" and "withheld capacity," whose full significance we shall endeavor to make clear later.

2
Participating idleness may arise under a restrictive quota scheme

"Participating idleness" in equipment is not always easily distinguishable as such in practice. Consider the case of machinery which is not working because of restrictive *quotas* imposed by a cartel in response to a fall of prices. Such equipment may remain unscrapped for various reasons. It is when its continued idle existence is due to the fear that quota rights will be lost if the capacity is exterminated, that participating idleness may arise. Participation rights may, of course, be obtained in other ways. For instance, arrangements *may* be come to enabling the plant to be scrapped. Compensation (in the form of a capital sum or its equivalent) may be paid to those who *exterminate* specialized productive capacity. But when compensation arrangements of this type are *not* resorted to, participating idleness is likely to occur.

3
Resources may actually attach themselves in idleness to a monopolized trade because of participation rights obtainable

The extreme form arises when resources are deliberately specialized—although it is recognized that they will remain idle—because, given the existing methods of determining quotas, the right to contribute a large output, or the right to continue with the present output, is thereby secured. The "quota" is, of course, always economically indeterminate.[2] But the associated interests must have *some* formula for distribution, however arbitrary, or the whole scheme for exploiting the community will break down. They can be observed in practice to fall back upon the idea of "reasonableness." According to this principle, the "just" output for any individual or firm seems to be one which stands in some relation to past output and existing capacity.[3] But each potentially competing enterprise which merges its interests within a restriction scheme will still endeavor to *enhance* its own rights within it. Hence a firm in this position will often insist upon retaining its capacity, or will even deliberately add to its capacity with a view to pleading for a bigger quota. In this way there arises one of the most interesting forms of "participating idleness." In the parallel case which concerns labor, we shall see that the distributive principle seems to be vaguely related to the equal moral right of each individual. This is absent in the case of the firm. Past output is frequently the apparent determining factor; but the amount of equipment possessed is also felt to give the right (on occasion, perhaps, the power) to contribute a certain output.

4

Unless complete mergers are possible, unused
capacity is likely to be maintained for "quota hunting"

Unused capacity of such a nature seems to be of consid-

---

[2] That is, there are no determinants in the price mechanism which apportion output among those who share in the benefits of monopoly. From the social standpoint the division must be arbitrary.

[3] On the question of "reasonableness" and the "just" quota, see HUTT, "Nature of Aggressive Selling," *Economica,* August 1935, pp. 315–16.

erable practical importance in the modern world. Several
economic phenomena typical of contemporary society arise
out of it. The struggle for a "just" distributive arrangement
among owners of potentially competing resources conflicts
with arrangements for the curbing of productive power. In
the case of a merger in which there is complete absorption
of all competitors or former interlopers, it appears to be
relatively easy to keep production in check and destroy
capacity. But with cartels, price rings and looser forms of
association, the interests which submit to collective control
are often reluctant and rebellious, threateningly dissatisfied
with their quotas. It is for this reason that "withheld capacity" is likely to be *preserved*. The retention of actual
capacity is expected to confer or to win rights of participation. And capacity may frequently be actually expanded for
the same reason, a process commonly alluded to as "allotment hunting" or "quota hunting."

5
*Since participating idleness militates
against harmonious output restriction, other
distributive arrangements may be sought*

With equipment, it is usually recognized, however, that
other distributive arrangements are possible. Indeed, there
may be a strong motive for such arrangements. There nearly
always exists the feeling that such "surplus capacity" ought
to be got rid of. It is recognized that the psychological effect
of large quantities of idle equipment militates against the
"loyal" maintenance of prices. When this point of view
asserts itself, another aspect of the idleness is coming to
light, namely, its *"aggressive"* potentialities. Now while, as
we shall see, the "aggressive" aspect strengthens the monop-

oly in that it defends it from external interlopers, the internal situation is frequently precarious unless the distributive scheme is accepted as patently just by all those who are subject to it. If it is not felt to be just, then each member with idle resources seems to be constantly menacing the rest. The mere existence of "participating idleness" in these circumstances may, therefore, prevent the preservation of good internal relations within an output-curtailing group, just as armaments intended to bring security to individual nations appear at times likely to precipitate war. So long as "excess capacity" exists, the cartel organizers have a delicate task. It follows that, when practicable, a sort of disarmament scheme is brought into effect. The actual scrapping or physical destruction of plant is arranged with a view to removing the incentive for "allotment hunting." Or, less drastically, internal financial arrangements lead to an agreement not to provide for depreciation or renewal of the less favorably situated plant, so that the "surplus capacity" is gradually wiped out. These *internal* quarrels between potentially competing interests are, however, always in danger of being patched up and the plundering of consumers given a greater measure of permanence. As peace is to the advantage of all nations considered collectively, so the preservation of the monopoly is to the advantage of the members of the restriction scheme considered collectively. If the members can only have confidence in one another's integrity, then the presence of "participating idleness" will bring no disadvantage over and above the loss of interest on the scrap value of the "withheld capacity"; and as we shall see later, the corresponding "aggressive" function in respect of interlopers from outside will make its continuance an advantage. It will not affect the immediate optimum price for the output of the monopolist group; but it will make a higher long-run optimum possible.

6

*Interloping resources may be attracted in
to share in the chance of employment in a monopolized
field. The consequent participating idleness may be
illustrated by the example of petrol retailing*

*   Possibly the most important cases of "participating idleness" are those in which there are no struggles for distributive rights other than the reliance upon a certain *chance* of sharing in the spoils. The condition may exist when there is no effective restriction on entry into a privileged field of production. The owners of the idle resources know that through their existence and disposition, a certain *chance* of sharing in the benefits of a particular restrictionism will be achieved. In this instance, therefore, no question of quotas arises. A good illustration of "participating idleness" of this type in equipment is found in the provision of petrol supply stations *when the retailers own or hire the apparatus*. Let us assume, for simplicity, that there is competition between the companies producing and supplying petrol (i.e., competition *except* among the retailers themselves) so that the virtually standard nature of petrol is recognized, and that therefore separate tanks and pumps for the different brands
*   of rival companies do not exist. Tacit or formal monopoly may still rule in the relations among the retailers themselves, and be expressed in tacit or formal price maintenance. If such relations have influenced the charge for retailing petrol in any district, and there have been no completely effective arrangements preventing interlopers from invading the mar-

ket, more equipment is likely to be provided than would have been set up under competition. For there are benefits to be reaped by participation in the monopoly revenues, and the mere provision of equipment confers the chance of sharing in them. Hence the process continues, successively diluting the shares obtained by each participant. The theoretical limit is set by the situation which exists when the chance of employment (the average degree of utilization) has fallen to an extent which equates the value of an investment in the monopolized field with an investment outside. Such a theoretical limit would tend to be approached only when interlopers could really intervene successfully; and if this were so, any *tacit* monopoly would break down. That is, unless custom or coercion fixed the price of petrol, it would fall to a level which would be inconsistent with any idle plant other than that in "pseudo-idleness" (the case discussed in Chapter III, paragraph 11). Contemporary social arrangements very seldom permit so economical a process, however, and a measure of participating idleness under which the earnings of exploitation are fairly widely diffused is the most common phenomenon in the retailing of petrol. The condition is manifested in more idleness or more scanty use being made of part or all of the plant than is required by the indivisibility of the efficient unit of apparatus.[4] There is some extra capacity which, in the absence of the price agreement or tacit understanding, it would never pay to provide. For, so long as the price maintenance persists, all interloping equipment renders unprofitable (*ceteris paribus*) the utilization of an exactly equal capacity (on the assumption, of course, that the most profitable output is known).

---

[4] Efficient, that is, in relation to any local concentration of demand.

In these circumstances, interlopers *insert* a quantum *into* the output of services; they do not *add to* the output.[5] An identical situation exists whenever we get that duplication or multiplication of plant which propagandist and other confused literature refers to as "the wastes of competition."[6]

7
Participating idleness may easily be confused with pseudo-idleness or aggressive idleness

We must recognize that in equipment the preservation of "excess capacity" under monopoly *may* often be due to other motives than the achievement of "participating" rights. It is difficult to interpret actual situations. "Pseudo-idleness," in particular, may be mistaken for "participating idleness." Thus, the associated owners of equipment may want to have it available at a later date because they think that a revival of demand will then make an expansion of output profitable. They may believe this, even if they have a complete monopoly of their specific product. And they are even more likely to be reluctant to give up (i.e., despecialize by scrapping) productive capacity if it is their policy to forestall the intervention of potential interlopers when better times arrive; for to pursue this policy they must not unduly exploit their monopoly in response to expanding demand, and they will then be glad to have the reserve plant available. But "aggressive idleness" is probably even more easily confused with "participating." We shall return to this question.

---

[5] See HUTT, "Nature of Aggressive Selling," *Economica*, August 1935, p. 315.

[6] We must remind the reader that if the geographical (spatial) distribution of demand plus the indivisibility of the efficient unit of apparatus causes intermittent utilization there is no wastefulness present. There is "pseudo-idleness."

Appendix

Notes and Comments on Chapter VII

In 1939 we still felt that there was no good reason to substitute that awful word "oligopoly"[1] for the time-honored term "tacit monopoly," although we ourselves slipped into using the term in Chapter X, paragraph 8. Since then, however, with much analytical examination of the concept, "oligopoly" has become an accepted part of the jargon of economics. Nevertheless, we have thought it best to keep to our resolve not to change the original text in any respect. 6

The reference in paragraph 6 to the confusion between the opposites of *protection of competitors* and *protection of competition* is as important today as it was in 1939. *Competitors* are protected through the *imposition* of restraints on the market, while the process of *competition* is protected through the *prevention or removal* of such restraints (through antitrust). The confusion is largely because of a fuzzy conception of the competitive process. The meaning 6

---

[1] This term was coined in 1934, we think, by Professor Joan Robinson in her very important *Economics of Imperfect Competition*.

of the term "competition" as a process is usually assumed to be obvious. In equilibrium analysis all economists accept its conventional representation as a horizontal demand curve, which *is* perfectly clear; but the *process* of competition occurs between persons and corporations and governments, and each is normally confronted with a downward-sloping short-run demand curve. We have defined the process of competition as follows:

> The process of competition is the "substitution of a lower cost method of (a) producing and marketing any commodity or service or (b) attaining any other objective (material or non-material, private or collective) which involves a cost (the sacrifice of any other commodity or valued objective), *irrespective of the institutional framework needed to create, or release and/or protect incentives for the substitution.*"[2]

This definition covers the case of a substitution of a preferred product. Now under such a definition how can competition ever be "wasteful" or "predatory"? But the price mechanism through which the valuation of ends and means required for the substitution process occurs can itself be used to frustrate the competitive process. The possible predatory use of pricing must therefore be faced. It is discussed in Chapter XI as "aggressive selling."[3]

---

[2] *Say's Law*, pp. 15–16.

[3] This is a topic which we first discussed in 1935 in *Economica*, "The Nature of Aggressive Selling."

Chapter VIII

Participating Idleness
in Labor

1

*Participating idleness in labor is most clear
under "short-time" work with "work-sharing" motives,
the monopoly revenues being shared equally*

"Participating idleness" in labor is found in its clearest   *
form in "short-time" labor policy with "work-sharing"
motives. By withholding labor, the workers receive a sum
over and above what would have been the competitive (natural scarcity) value of the total work supplied. But instead
of some of the workers moving out to other jobs when the
amount of work supplied is thus cut down, they participate
in the extra revenues by sharing in the reduced supply of
work. *Sharing the work confers the right to share the spoils.*
If they move out, they lose such rights: hence they stay, in
partial idleness. Having once obtained a footing in the trade,
they can claim their share by exploiting the supposed moral
sanction of the "right to work." This means an equal share
of the revenues per individual, for such equality is regarded
as obviously equitable.[1]

---

[1] The rights are not taken as completely equal where the question of grades

2
Cessation of recruitment is a means of
sharing monopoly revenues among a declining number

*   As those attached to a trade which has "withheld capacity" die off, however, their rights tend to die with them; and if things remain static, the monopoly revenues will gradually come to be shared among a smaller number of individuals. But other things do not remain static in practice. External causes can be observed to lead to the breakdown of this form of protectionism. Moreover, even when the restrictions are most strong, it may be felt that the sons of those employed, for instance, also have the "right to work." And public opinion, which has to be considered, is influenced by the search for careers. Sufficient apprenticeship or recruitment will sometimes be permitted, therefore, to spread the proceeds over a number of individuals which does not diminish. But the existence of "short-time" usually seems to justify the refusal to recruit. And there is no necessary reason why those with control of entry should not limit recruitment until, following deaths and departures, all attached to the trade are employed for the full conventional working day, while sharing the plunder among themselves. The monopoly continues, but "participating idleness" has then vanished.

3
Participating rights are not conferred
on a worker accepting another employment

Now, curiously enough, the point of view which regards an equal division of the monopoly revenues as obviously

---

comes in. If the proportionate numbers of workers in each grade (e.g., between bricklayers and their laborers) can be rigidly enforced, there can be *any* division of the spoils between the groups as such.

equitable almost always vanishes if an individual does not remain in the actual employment. We say "curiously" because no imaginable equity would be disturbed if an individual could carry such rights with him. Distributive arrangements are *conceivable* under which the smaller supply of work could be provided by a smaller number of workers, each working for the full working day, the rest leaving the trade and getting their proportion of the proceeds of exploitation in the form of compensation. The burden on the community would be less if that course were followed, for the workers withdrawing could compete (i.e., society could utilize their services) in other fields. But we have found no case of this in practice. Either there has been no recognition of the surplus of monopolistic earnings over competitive earnings under labor restrictionism;[2] or, if the surplus has been clearly or dimly recognized, it has been felt that public opinion would not approve of more blatant ways of dividing it up.

4

An excluded worker may remain
unemployed and attached to a monopolized trade
because his availability increases his chance
of the privileged employment it may offer

A rather similar and fairly common case is that which originates when a worker is *ousted* from his trade through an enforced wage-rate increase (which makes his continued employment unprofitable) or through wage-rate rigidity in

---

[2] This is most frequently the explanation. The workers themselves, of course, do not recognize that they are in any sense sharing in the benefits of restrictionism. In the usual case, they may simply know that they have found the field which gives them the best attainable income.

times of depression. Work sharing is not thought to be good policy and the benefits are held on to by those who are actually employed. Let us suppose also that there is no *partial* sharing through unemployment benefit. The ousted worker may then refuse other available work, not (as in the case of "pseudo-idleness") because the *competitive* rate of earnings in his original trade makes his *chance* of employment there more valuable, but because his *chance* of sharing in the monopoly gains is thereby increased. If he has once been in the trade, his chance of this is higher than if he is *purely* an interloper. For, although his right to share equally in the spoils has been tacitly denied, it may still seem morally just that increased demand for the product should result in his being absorbed before any *further* exploitation of consumers should be practiced. His availability is, so to speak, privileged.

5
*Even if temporary employment would not
destroy an excluded worker's availability it might
weaken his* right *to privileged employment*

The amount of idleness may be enhanced in such a situation because the displaced worker is likely to regard it as good tactics to refuse other employments even when they do not reduce his actual availability in case of a revival of demand. For unless he has priority rights obtained through membership of a skilled union, the possession of another job may seem to weaken the force of his "right to work" in his former occupation. This factor probably works in very closely with another psychological consideration. The displaced worker may know that he will "lose caste" through accepting lowly paid work temporarily and that this will militate against his return to his main occupation. Thus J. S. Poyntz tells us[3] how "one foreman says that a mechanic who is out of work would not go to the gasworks in the winter; he believes that he would rather starve. It would count against him in his next job. They would say, 'He is only a gasstoker; he is no mechanic.' " In part, such refusal of work must be regarded as coming under the category of "preferred idleness," in that the feared loss of prestige is a fear of the loss of *amour propre.* The loss of the *right* to work (or the right to priority in recruitment) as a mechanic may, however, often be the main factor in this kind of circumstance.

6

Interlopers may be attracted in *to share in
the* chance *of employment in a monopolized field.
The consequent participating idleness may be
illustrated by the example of stockbrokers*

"Participating idleness" of the type in which there is no struggle for distributive rights other than the reliance upon a certain chance of sharing in the spoils arises not only through those eliminated from employment in a trade remaining attached to it, but through interlopers actually being attracted in. When it is present, we have one of the circumstances in which the term "overcrowded," as applied to an occupation, has some meaning. The state can occur when the remuneration of those in a trade is fixed monopolistically at a high rate, while freedom of entry cannot be completely prevented, or priority of recruitment cannot be effectively enforced. The clearest example is that of stockbrokers whose charges are fixed while entry is only partially

---

[3] In WEBB and FREEMAN, op. cit., p. 48.

restricted. Many stockbrokers have little business to do for quite long periods, but owing to the absence of competition, there is still a sufficient chance of earnings to make it worth their while to enter and remain.

7
Participating idleness in the medical profession

*   In other professions, the participating idleness or idling is not so simply demonstrable. A complex and possibly important example is that of medicine. There are some grounds for fearing that the problem will become serious at some future time in this profession. But the situation is disguised in this case. Fees for medical services are not fixed as stockbrokers' charges are fixed. There is, indeed, nothing to prevent a doctor from practicing discriminatory charges as between his patients. But this power in itself proves the existence of some personal, or collective professional monopoly; and although not formally fixed, fees are controlled by "reasonableness" (tacit monopoly), custom (differing from district to district), understandings, and notions of professional etiquette. There is no "standard rate," but the trade union is powerful. On the other hand, the limitation of entrance through heavy charges for training, lengthy courses of study, and a process of elimination by examination cannot be completely effective. For apart from the possibility that public opinion would revolt against too conspicuous a restriction of entry, there are vested interests on the part of teaching institutions which can collect a tax for the privilege of competing for entry to the profession. The teaching interests are not likely to allow this valuable traffic to be killed by the practicing interests. There is also rivalry among the teaching bodies which weakens the tacit monopoly that gives rise to the tax. Fees for tuition and training are not so high as they could otherwise be fixed, and the percentage of passes at examinations is allowed to be higher. The result is that in the profession itself a system of sharing (of both work and remuneration) must sooner or later come into being, many practitioners earning a living more by the height of their fees than by the intensity of their work. The effects of overcrowding in this case would be seen in a certain leisureliness, or slackness, or padding, on the part of many practitioners; not in actual "idleness" in the usual connotation of that term. We may call the condition "participating idling."[4] As long as means of entry are not made too difficult or expensive, this dilution, both of services performed and of the monopoly revenues, is likely to continue. Eventually, after successive dilutions, individual expectations of earnings within the profession must reach an equilibrium (a dangerously unstable equilibrium, perhaps) with those in other occupations. This equilibrium will depend upon the presence of underwork—a diffused and disguised[5] "withheld capacity"—in the protected profession.

---

[4] The fact that the leisureliness is not evenly spread (as it would tend to be if chance were the *only* factor) is due partly to the fact that differential reputation, social standing, personality (and perhaps differential skill), and the good will which is bought with a practice, and so forth, influence the amount of services rendered by individuals at the conventional or fixed fees.

[5] Thus, consultations may take longer than would really represent economy of a practitioner's time if he were trying to work at full capacity. This is one of the results of the situation which always arises when prices are fixed but not the output and quality of the commodity sold. Competition then tends to be expressed in other, less urgent things than prices (from the consumers' point of view).

8
Participating idleness may exist in poorly paid casual trades

*   Something of the same situation can exist in some of the casual and very poorly paid trades. Difficulty arises in studying this province, however, for in the interpretation of practice, we are faced with a very complex situation. In the first place, such employments are already "overcrowded" in a sense different from that which is implied by our term "participating idleness." As we have emphasized earlier, badly paid occupations represent the opportunities left to all those who have been excluded from better ones by restrictionism in the labor market. Hence, rates of earnings are likely to be very low in the remaining opportunities *even if there is additional restrictionism* in them. Secondly, and this is a more serious problem, with which we must deal, there may be no *obvious* monopolization but yet *actual* monopolization among workers in the least privileged types of occupation. In the absence of wage fixation (say by trade boards), it may seem that we have absolutely no parallel to the cases of "participating idleness" which we have already discussed. But a similar situation may in fact arise for the reasons explained in the following paragraph.

9
The odium attaching to employers of low-paid labor has the same consequence as wage fixation

*   In the matter of the remuneration of the lowest paid sections of the working classes, a thoroughly confused public opinion tends to view with disfavor those who offer employment to workers whose services are of low market value.

Instead of condemning practices and institutions which *cause* their value to be low, it is customary to frown on the *entrepreneurs* through whose initiative they are connected with the most satisfactory remaining opportunities. Consider the common reprobation of "the sweater," for instance. So stupid have typical reformers been, that they have expected *petty* capitalists, as well as important ones, to rectify a situation which is the product of widespread restrictionism. The whole system of distribution through the value mechanism has been influenced by coercive interferences in the labor market; and yet the "sweater" (the "bad employer") has been expected to put this right by paying more than the market rate for the dregs of the labor supply. Thus, when a "national minimum" has been advocated (on the grounds that great poverty is deplorable) the plea has not been for *distributive* arrangements to enable the community to pay (through taxation) for pensions or bonuses for the poor, which would remove the social conditions or injustices that offend it.[6] On the contrary, the agitations have been unwittingly asking for production to be cut down (i.e., for scarcities to be contrived) in unmonopolized fields; for such is, of course, the actual effect of burdening any set of free productive operations with imposed costs. The poor are to be helped by the taxation of those who supply co-

---

[6] In other ways, such direct redistribution *is* resorted to, especially through the "social services." A good example is the case of subsidized housing schemes. But here the benefits in practice go to those organized in building rings, the suppliers of building materials, architects and privileged artisans. This appears to work to the actual detriment of the poor, as the subventions have the effect of bolstering the various building monopolies. With the education services, professional parasitism has not been so effective and some part of the benefits have been allowed to reach the poor.

operant resources for the employment of the ousted poor, and by consumers being made to bear a wholly avoidable detriment. And as in general the poorest must also suffer most as consumers, and as those who are not poor usually manage to get part of the proceeds of contrived scarcities (especially "the good employers"),[7] the ultimate result is to rob the underdog of much more than is conspicuously distributed to him. It is widespread confusion of this kind which has led to the tragically misconceived antisweating propaganda and it is the same confusion which is indirectly responsible for "participating idleness" in the low-wage classes. It has meant that odium has attached to the employers of the poor. Hence, when "the employers" have been large corporations with some measure of "natural monopoly"; or when they have stood in tacit monopoly relation to their rivals (like, say, the London Dock companies in prewar times), and when their managements have also been sensitive to public feeling; or when the humanitarianism of their directors has not been guided by social insight; they may have voluntarily offered wage-rates in excess of the market value of labor and so have burdened their economy with extra costs, restricted their demand for labor and recouped themselves from the consumer. In spite of the cause being misplaced altruism on the part of the employing corporations, or their conspicuous if reluctant response to public disapproval of low wage-rates, the effect in these circumstances is exactly the same as if wage fixation had been resorted to by labor combinations or authoritarian action. Whether the origin of the policy is mainly altruistic

---

[7] On the significance of "the good employers," protected by wage fixation, see HUTT, *Theory of Collective Bargaining,* pp. 100–4.

or due to fear of odium is of no consequence. The *fact* must be recognized if the complexities of the unskilled labor market are to be realistically studied.[8]

10
Participating idleness is an important contributory cause of the casual nature of some poorly paid employments. In these circumstances, decasualization is inequitable

We have to face, therefore, a curious result. A trade in which earnings would be regarded as low even under continuous employment for the conventional working day may yet be remunerated at so much above the market rate that, when all attached to it have a roughly equal chance of being taken on each day or each week, a sufficient number will share in that employment to reduce the average earnings of the marginal employees to what they could earn elsewhere. Surely this is an important contributory cause of "casual labor." If this "participation" factor is the sole cause in any case, then the recurrent idleness of individuals cannot be regarded as the productive condition which can be called a "reserve." The remedy in such a situation cannot be the

---

[8] There can be an additional cause of "participating idleness" associated with casual labor in a field in which there is free entry. When it is difficult for "the employers" to judge individual efficiency, it is very easy for tacit monopoly to arise among the workers employed. It will be expressed as "participating idling," in the form of *ca' canny*—not necessarily organized, but a spontaneous, hardly collusive withholding of efficiency with the immediate object of increasing the chance of employment—of making the job last as long as possible. But unless there is a barrier to the occupation, or unless there are no poorer classes capable of interloping, each extension of monopoly will result in a countervailing dilution, again until the *expectation of earnings* within is equated to that outside.

arrangement of an imposed or collusive decasualization, unless those responsible for policy are prepared to enforce a less equitable division of the opportunities which the labor market offers. The reformer might regard that solution as the lesser of two evils. But, to be defensible, imposed or collusive decasualization ought to be advocated only after the fullest recognition has been given to these considerations.

11
Work-sharing arrangements resemble the quota systems of cartels; and unemployment benefits paid out of union funds resemble cartel bonuses to compensate for the withdrawal of output

There is a very close analogy between cartel practice and current trade union policy in the device of "short time." In so far as the latter represents deliberate work-sharing, it brings about a kind of underemployment similar to the effects of reduced quota allotments when the equipment, although having scrap value, is not scrapped. We have seen that alternative arrangements enabling participation in the spoils of restrictionism are conceivable. Such arrangements appear to exist under a trade union's unemployment fund, or under an unemployment insurance scheme in which the funds are provided entirely by the workers' own contributions. The object of unemployment pay is undoubtedly in part to secure the consent of those whose labor is displaced by high wage policy. They are potential interlopers, dangerous to the monopoly; and unemployment pay certainly makes their acquiescence more likely, or renders easier their loyalty to the unions in the advantages of whose restrictions they themselves may hope to share later on. The resemblance to the bonuses paid by some cartels for the idleness of certain plants is obvious.

12
Unlike unemployment benefits, cartel bonuses
are not contingent upon the continued idleness of the
resources in alternative employments

But the existence of unemployment pay does not result in practice in the dissolution of "participating idleness" among displaced workers. This constitutes a possibly important distinction between the endowment of "withheld capacity" in plant and its endowment in labor. The factory owner who accepts a reduced quota (in return for a bonus) is free, if he wishes, to apply his "redundant" plant to some noncompeting work: the displaced worker is *not allowed* to use his powers in other fields. Private and State unemployment insurance benefits are in practice virtually contingent upon the individual refusing any paid work, even outside the trade from which his colleagues have ejected him or from which he has "loyally" withdrawn. Moreover, similar conditions are insisted upon in respect of State and private philanthropic "poor relief." "Participating" rights in these circumstances are dependent upon virtually absolute idleness. Possibly because those responsible for policy are inhibited from regarding such contributions as bonuses for scarcity creation—the frank recognition of which might cause disconcerting misgivings in respect of the morality of the policy; or possibly because, in contrast with work sharing, the distribution of the advantages or the incidence of the burden will seem unjust; or perhaps because of other sources of confusion which cause the contributions to be regarded as charitable payments, generously subscribed by warm-hearted colleagues; the workers displaced by labor restrictionism are given, not unconditional compensation to make up their income to something near to what they could earn a free market, but a bounty for keeping out of the labor market altogether. The idleness resulting must be regarded as "participating" in spite of the distributive rights acquired happening to confer such a very meager portion.

13
In practice, State-subsidized unemployment benefits support general restrictionism in the labor market and are contingent upon absolute idleness

The position is complicated in practice because it is not only their union, or an organization representing "the industry" which buys the consent of displaced workers. The State also contributes. However admirable we may consider the political ideals which lead to the State contributing to unemployment funds, or however expedient we may consider the policy, we must admit that the effect is to provide an official support to private restrictionism in the labor market.[9] Society, unconsciously—and given the past perhaps wisely—accepting the goodness of the *status quo,* endeavors to preserve the rates of earnings among the more favored groups of workers; and the pacification of those displaced is seen to be a more effective way of preserving traditional inequalities than wage fixations alone.

---

[9] Postwar developments in England were realistically forecast by Sir Sydney Chapman in 1908. He pointed out how the subsidizing of trade-union insurance would eventually necessitate the State upholding trade-union policies and standards. (BRASSEY and CHAPMAN, *Work and Wages,* vol. II, pp. 325–36.)

14
Cartel arrangements are voluntary
in a sense in which labor restrictions are not

As the effect of unemployment insurance is in some measure a purchase of the cooperation of workers in a system which deprives them of the right to the more remunerative forms of work, we must regard their displacement as giving rise to "withheld capacity." It is less easy to regard it as "enforced idleness." At the same time we have to remember that the trade unionism or wage regulation which brings about their exclusion is not voluntary in the sense that cartel agreements are voluntary. The latter are usually rational agreements. Cartel members insist upon adequate bonuses in return for their promise not to undercut. But to an impartial and dispassionate observer it seems, on the face of it, that displaced workers get (from their union or the State) a mere sop. They appear to consent because they do not understand. The impression persistently asserts itself in the present writer's mind that it is nothing but their ignorance which prevents them from insisting upon an *equal* sharing of the spoils in return for their agreement to refrain from "blacklegging." They apparently acquiesce; the unanimous voice of their teachers has, one feels, instructed them that the restriction of competition constitutes their great safeguard; but the question of the distribution of the benefits of such restriction is never raised. Surely the acquiescence of the unemployed is based on an illusion which survives only because it is to no one's interest to dispel it. During the protests against "the means test" in Great Britain, this fundamental issue remained hidden.

15
For justice, the compensation conferred
by a union's unemployment pay should be complete

That the true nature of unemployment insurance is that of a bonus which is similar to, but in one crucial respect different from, the reward paid to a member of a price ring who cooperates by ceasing to contribute to output, has received hardly any recognition in the printed word. Blindness to this compensatory aspect of the "dole" has certainly colored the current moral attitude toward it in a quite unjustifiable manner. We can illustrate this point from a recent book by Professor Knoop. He appears to be arguing against subsidiary employment being undertaken by those in receipt of unemployment insurance benefits. Of course, Professor Knoop is justified in deploring any breach of the law. Yet one feels that his attitude is dictated by his acceptance of the view that "the dole" should rightly be, not compensation, but a charitable payment to those for whom no other work whatsoever is available. Consider the following passage. He says that ". . . the Insurance Fund is being bled for purposes which ought not to be possible. For example, a suburban grocer, with a trade almost entirely concentrated on Fridays and Saturdays, may be paying his assistant 42/- per week. If such assistant were suspended from Monday to Thursday inclusive, he could draw 4 days' benefit which in the case of a married man with one child would amount to 18/8d. The grocer might pay 25/- for his work on Friday and Saturday, so that the assistant would actually be better off than when on full work."[10] But why object to this? The

---

[10] D. KNOOP, *Riddle of Unemployment*, p. 166.

ideal would surely be for the grocer to employ this man for the Friday and Saturday only for 25/- and leave him free to serve the community in some other regular job from Monday to Thursday, or in the almost unlimited casual employment for which the individual can bid in a free labor market. Could we *then* say that the grocer was "bleeding" the community? Could we in any way deplore *his* action when the shop assistant to whom *he* gives a regular two days' work each week is paid 19/8d. out of the insurance fund on condition that he does not undertake *other* available work? And as for the shop assistant himself, if we bring in these moral issues, has he not a moral right to be "actually better off" than he would be if he depended on earnings alone? For has he not been ousted from, or persuaded to withhold his labor from the (individually) most profitable fields? We admit that many people will indignantly deny that the "ideal system" would leave such a person free to bid for whatever regular or casual work happened to be going during the first four days of the week. That, they will say, would cause him to compete and so to lower rates of earnings where they were already low. But if they argue this way, ought they not to contend also that compensation should be complete? If the leaders of organized labor really believe that "withheld capacity" generally practiced (taking the form of trade union or State wage fixation in the actual world, of course) can increase the earnings of the working classes as a whole, surely it is up to them to arrange an equitable system of sharing the benefits with those whom they force out of employment or persuade to withhold their labor. It is no answer to blame "the capitalist system." This sort of injustice is obviously rectifiable in the present.

16
Complete compensation would be insisted upon if the members of a trade union regarded it as shareholders do a firm

There would be a different story to tell if the members of a union regarded that body as shareholders do a firm. Displaced workers would then insist upon work sharing or *full* compensation. Such an enforced dilution of monopoly increments might, of course, give added strength to the motives which make trade unions into closed corporations. It is possible that patrimony, favoritism and bribery would be more powerful factors determining entrance to the better paid trades, and that age would repress youth, and men repress women, with even greater fervor. But the assertion of their rights by displaced unionists would also be likely to expose to the unprivileged classes the nature of the parasitism which condemns them to relative poverty.

17
Organized labor has usually been hostile to the dilution of monopoly revenues through work sharing

One feels that it has been a hazy recognition of such a threat to popular acquiescence in trade unionism that has stimulated occasional opposition to "short-time" policy from the industrial and political labor camps. The arguments used have, of course, stressed the unfairness to the workers themselves; the injustice of placing the burden on those least able to bear it; the danger that incomes generally will be forced below the minimum required for the maintenance of physical efficiency; and other considerations which the social scientist cannot help suspecting have been devised to camouflage the real issue. It is very interesting to notice the "complete right about face"[11] on the part of Mr. Sidney Webb on the short-time question. In 1891, it was clearly the "withheld capacity" aspect of the practice which had caught his attention. He then stressed (in *The Eight-Hour Day*) the "beneficial results" in respect of employment creation achieved through shorter hours. But by 1912 he could argue (at the National Conference on the Prevention of Destitution) that "a reduction of the hours of labor could not do anything whatsoever to prevent the occurrence of unemployment." Are we wrong in surmising that the "dilution" aspect of short time was now in Mr. Webb's mind, with all its menacing and ominous implications?

18
The failure of the poor to share their poverty is the most neglected aspect of the unemployment problem

If those social reformers who have no political or financial   *
ax to grind could only be brought to realize that their strivings would be better guided if the light of economic analysis were allowed to fall on the labor market which they try to explore, they might see a new problem. We believe that they would recognize the fact that the poor do not share their poverty as the most worrying and neglected aspect of unemployment as a labor problem. The incidence of unemployment, even when of the type which we class as "preferred idleness," is one expression of the unjust distribution[12] of

---

[11] So described by F. C. MILLS in *Contemporary Theories of Unemployment* (pp. 98–99, footnote), from which the following passages from Mr. Sidney Webb are quoted.

[12] "Unjust" in the sense of *unequal*.

the direct burdens of restrictionism. It is part of the wider issue of the inequitable sharing among the workers of their aggregate earnings. Because each class tries to be parasitic upon the class beneath it (in the wholly false belief that it is the capitalist class which is in fact mulcted), and because some compensation or relief is offered by society, distributive injustices are largely manifested in "preferred idleness."

Appendix

Notes and Comments on Chapter VIII

The phrase "right to work" as used in paragraph 1 means   1
almost the opposite of the same phrase as used in the
United States since the Taft-Hartley Act. The former means
the right of a person to share in the remuneration of a particular kind of work, even when he contributes no inputs:
the latter refers to the right of any person to accept any job
offer which he believes may improve his earnings, conditions
of work, or prospects. In paragraph 2, the former notion is   2
extended to union patrimony—a son's right to share in a
union's spoils of exploitation when his father is or was a
member of the union.

Our example in paragraph 7 of "participating idleness"   7
in the medical profession (and especially the reference to "a
certain leisureliness or slackness" on the part of the practitioners) must seem highly unrealistic unless the reader
remembers our deliberately unrealistic assumption that the
"means of entry" to the profession "are not made too difficult or expensive." In the United States, where the author
has lived for a decade, the costs and difficulties of entry

appear to be purposely formidable, while the practitioners work at high intensity, demand much leisure, and tend to retire early.

8   Paragraph 8 treats of the participating idleness phenomenon among workers driven into or confined to "sub-optimal employments" ("disguised unemployment"). The 1939 text does not sufficiently stress this.

"Trade boards" were British wage-determining tribunals in certain nonunionized occupations with relatively low remuneration. They were constituted of "employers" and "employees" and "neutral" members. They were custommade for "joint monopoly" in sub-optimal production.[1]

9   Dealing with subsidies (paragraph 9, footnote 6), we contrast building subsidies with education subsidies. The former, we suggest, do *not* reduce the price of housing but increase profits and wages in the building trade; whereas subsidies of education do cheapen it, even to the extent of providing it "free," instead of merely raising teachers' salaries. But in 1939 we were dealing with a period in which the teaching profession was not unionized as it is today. In the present age (in the United States at any rate) teachers' strikes have forced taxpayers to increase the subsidy almost entirely for the private benefit of the teachers.

9   The term "ca' canny" is an old Scottish term (taken over by the British) for "work sharing"—going slow in the belief that the employment can be made to last longer.

18   We feel now that the last five lines of paragraph 18 are not well phrased. Although labor unions are, in fact, parasitic upon those with incomes lower than those of their own members, and apparently indifferent to the relative poverty

---

[1] See HUTT, *Collective Bargaining*, 2d ed., pp. 20, 23, 55, 67–72, 86, 102.

they cause and perpetuate, we ought not to have suggested that they *know* they are parasitic in that sense. But our contention that they act "in the wholly false belief that it is the capitalist class which is in fact mulcted" is justified. We have tried elsewhere to explain the sense in which investors are unexploitable through the private use of coercive power.[2] Briefly, *marginal prospective yields to investment in the retention, replacement or net accumulation of assets in different productive activities tend to equality irrespective of their vulnerability to strike-threat exploitation.*

[2] Ibid.; *Strike-Threat,* especially chapters 1, 10, 11, 15 and 16.

Chapter IX

Enforced Idleness

1

*Resources excluded from or withheld from
monopolized employments must, if they remain idle,
be idle in some other sense also*

There is another aspect of all resources which are in a state of "participating idleness" and of some which are idle in other senses. As any increment of resources which is in "participating idleness" could secure employment at any moment in the monopolized field by the process of under-cutting, it must either be "forced" into idleness or be voluntarily "withheld." We can distinguish, therefore, two broad aspects of "participating idleness"; it is either "enforced idleness" or it is "withheld capacity." These self-explanatory terms have already been used, but must now be further considered. They indicate causes of idleness just as the term "participating" does. If the enforcement is removed, or the motive to withhold is dissolved, the idleness disappears; and, on the other side, the loss of the "participating" rights or their conferment in other ways, will also cause the resources to be utilized, through scrapping or otherwise, in new fields.

"Participating idleness" is not, however, the only form of idleness which results from coercion or the withholding of capacity. In the case of labor, the excluded or withheld resources may be left in a state of "preferred idleness"; and in the case of all excluded or withheld resources, they may be left in a state of "valuelessness" *in respect of any alternative employments* (absence of net scrap value when equipment is concerned), or in a state of "pseudo-idleness" *in respect of any alternative employments.* It is clear, therefore, that the exclusion or withholding of resources is never a *complete* explanation of their idleness. They must either be "valueless" for all other uses or be left idle in some other sense.

2

Enforced idleness is caused by the exclusion
of resources during the monopolization of production;
but the term has a limited meaning

*   Enforced idleness exists when specialized resources (*a*) have been driven out of one productive employment by legal enactments (fixing prices, or fixing output directly), by physical violence, by threats, by "moral suasion," by strikes, by boycotts, or by the use or threatened use of discriminatory charges (as under "aggressive selling") and yet (*b*) have not taken other employments because of some "participating" rights conferred by idleness, or for one of the other reasons we have mentioned. Hence the notion of "enforced idleness" has a limited meaning. It does not refer to resources which have been diverted from any employment by restrictionism, unless they are then idle for one of these additional reasons. Thus, workers who have been deprived of their customary jobs (for which they have acquired specialized skill) through the raising of wage-rates, or the maintenance of wage-rates in times of depression, do not come into this category unless they refuse to accept alternative employments. And plants which are forced to shut down because of charges imposed on their economy through restrictive industrial legislation[1] can only be reckoned as examples of "enforced idleness" if they remain in existence. We cannot usefully think of their scrap materials (directed to the next best employment) as "idle."

3
*Enforced idleness must be distinguished from
two other forms of "waste": (i) specialized "diverted
resources" which happen to find inferior employments, and
(ii) the hypothetical resources which might have become
specialized in the monopolized field but for
powers of exclusion*

Although, in a sense, those who have been prevented   * from acquiring skill in any trade because of apprenticeship regulations or irrelevant educational requirements may be thought of as "excluded," we cannot regard them as in "enforced idleness." Nor can we bring into this category those who are kept from a trade, for which they could acquire competence, by some trade union demarcation, or sex bar or color bar, unless they had at some time enjoyed employment in it. Similarly, we cannot regard physical resources which would have become specialized for a particular employment in the absence of restrictive legislation or private coercion as representing a sort of hypothetical

---

[1] Industrial legislation preserving some collective good obviously does not fall under the heading of "restrictive," e.g., laws preventing the pollution of rivers or the atmosphere.

"enforced idleness." When we think of "idleness" in one of the senses in which the condition can be deplored, it is simply a conception which enables us to distinguish the most conspicuous (certainly not the most serious) forms of waste from others. It helps us to envisage the nature of a particular set of symptoms of waste. Capital equipment, driven into subsidiary, makeshift uses under "planning" and such-like policies designed to secure "prosperity" represents what may be called "diverted resources"; but resources which become specialized to inferior productive fields because of the power of exclusion cannot be called "diverted." They represent waste in yet another sense. All monopolies —in other words, all *contrived scarcities*—involve enforced *waste;* but the different forms of idleness can only be *indications* of its presence. The absence of idleness does not imply the absence of waste. In searching for the reasons which result in *the manifestation of waste in idleness,* it is appropriate to connect the causes with the immediate acts of public or private policy that precipitate it. Hence it is profitable to distinguish between (*a*), "enforced idleness," and (*b*), (i) "diverted resources" which (while specialized) find fields of utilization, and (ii) hypothetical resources (including those whose original specialization might have been appropriate but has been destroyed by scrapping) which might have become specialized in the monopolized field but for coercive or voluntary powers of exclusion. At what point the process of despecialization causes resources to pass from class (i) to class (ii) is not important. But the main distinction—between (*a*) and (*b*)—is important because "frictional unemployment" and "technological unemployment" are commonly regarded as due in part to demarcations and rigid wage-rates which restrict mobility between not greatly dissimilar occupations. But while these things cause the *diversion* of resources, and deter otherwise profitable specialization, they need not, in themselves, precipitate "enforced idleness." And the most serious productive developments which are deterred through the exercise of monopoly power find no manifestation either as "diverted resources" whose specialization remains, or as resources in "enforced idleness."

4

"Diverted labor resources" may be described
as in "disguised unemployment," but the condition
is unimportant in relation to other forms of waste
which are not expressed in idleness

Now Mrs. Robinson[2] has suggested that it is desirable to describe as "unemployed" certain resources which fall into the "diverted resources" category. She suggests that we should say that those workers are in "disguised unemployment" who have lost their main occupation and, although in jobs which produce *some* earnings, are virtually unemployed from a realistic standpoint. If we have correctly understood her point, it is that their meager incomes merely hide or disguise what is most important in their condition. For conceivable practical problems, her term is, perhaps, serviceable and graphic. There is waste of capacity and a distributive injustice in such a situation, and statistical and empirical studies of "unemployment" can easily ignore this aspect of the condition of the "employed" population. But the evil in this case is not *idleness,* and doubts as to the

---

[2] *Economic Journal*, 1937, p. 266; *Essays in the Theory of Unemployment,* p. 82.

appropriateness of the term "disguised unemployment" arise therefore. Nevertheless, if we confine the notion to "diverted *labor* resources" which have been driven into some inferior occupation it may have some usefulness. The inferior occupation must involve the nonutilization of specialization (i.e., natural or acquired skill relevant to a particular task) which would still have value under free exchange in the *original occupation*. The conception connects the excluded workers with an employment into which they could immediately *slip back* if the coercion were broken down or (as we shall see in the following chapter) if the motive to withhold their labor disappeared. It cannot helpfully apply to wasted productive power which has not been "diverted," however. There is no "disguised idleness" in the nonutilization of the *potential* capacities of the labor force in trades to which they have never been allowed to "become attached"; and *it is this last effect which really constitutes the serious waste under restrictive wage and recruitment policies*. Thus, working-class women may have become specialized to household duties largely through the exclusiveness of men's labor organization. But although excluded from well-paid employments, there is no waste of *specialized* capacity; they have not been "diverted" in our sense. Hence they could not be regarded as in "disguised unemployment." Even if many such women could be *immediately* employed as interlopers at cut rates in unskilled jobs now monopolized by men, they would not be in "disguised unemployment"; for they would never have become "attached to" those trades. Their existing powers would be wasted but not "diverted." The essence of "diverted resources," which we may call "disguised unemployment" in the case of labor, is that a reversal of policy would enable the specialized resources to slip back into their first use. But we must repeat that such cases of wasteful utilization are not important in relation to the aggregate wastefulness in the application of, and the process of specialization of, productive power. Just as wasteful idleness indicates the presence of, but by no means expresses the burden of, the curbing of productive power, so "diverted resources" must form a very small, if perceptible, proportion of all wasted resources.

5
*Enforced idleness may be caused by the
monopolization of cooperant stages of production*

We must also regard as falling into "enforced idleness" those specialized resources in "participating idleness," or those which are "valueless," the original demand for which has declined subsequently to the investment owing to some contrived scarcity in respect of cooperant resources. In other words, not only may collusion among competitors enforce idleness, but the monopolization of a cooperant stage of production may have the same result. Thus, if there is a small gasworks which earns just enough to pay for prime costs, a rise in the price of coal owing to a cooperative coal marketing policy may force it to cease operations. Idleness in that sense is "enforced" also. The position becomes very complicated in this type of case, however (i.e., when it is cooperant and not competing resources which are excluded by monopolistic policy). For the *entrepreneur's* decisions in the process affected may also be giving effect to some *new withholding* of capacity which he judges to be profitable because of the contrived scarcity in the cooperant stages of production. Or the idleness may be in the nature of a strike (although not popularly recognizable as such) due to a quarrel about the division of revenues obtained by joint restrictionism. But monopoly in respect of one process (which may or may not involve "enforced idleness" or "withheld capacity" in the resources specialized for it)[3] may undoubtedly enforce idleness in specialized resources devoted to cooperant processes. As Professor Knoop has pointed out, "because wages are forced up in some sheltered industry, it does not follow that that industry will be the one to experience unemployment; the prejudicial consequences may affect other industries. For example, high wages in the railway industry, by helping to keep up railway rates, may react unfavorably on the coal industry and the iron and steel industry, in both of which cost of carriage is an important item among the expenses."[4]

---

[3] Obviously monopoly does not involve "idleness" when resources have been deterred from specializing themselves for the monopolized production.

[4] D. KNOOP, *Riddle of Unemployment*, p. 128.

Appendix

Notes and Comments on Chapter IX

Our reference in paragraph 2 to resources "driven out of
one productive employment . . . by strikes" may mislead because, in the modern world, "threats to strike" or even "the right to strike" are far more important than actual strikes. In the peaceful, courteous, almost diplomatic atmosphere of typical wage negotiations today, the word "strike" need never be heard, but the threat to strike is there —"the gun under the table," as it has been graphically described.

In mentioning "restrictive industrial legislation" in this paragraph we ought to have laid more stress today on the very important point made in footnote 1, namely, that legally enacted regulations for the conduct of productive operations, when aimed at the attainment of collectively sought objectives such as industrial health and safety, unpolluted air or water, cannot be regarded as necessarily "restrictive." Such objectives, acquired at a sacrifice of other objectives, including the sacrifice of other commodities, are themselves commodities produced at a cost. The fact that the benefits the community purchases through such regulations may often, for many reasons, not be judged as worth their cost (the sacrifice involved), does not affect the point at issue. As individuals also, we may purchase foolishly.

3   What we describe in the heading of paragraph 3, and in the text, as "diverted resources," or as "disguised idleness of resources," are, we remind the reader, men and assets forced into or confined to "sub-optimal employments." The advantage of the phrase "sub-optimal employments" over those of "diverted resources" and "disguised idleness" of resources is that the former covers resources *excluded from* more remunerative activities as well as those *displaced from* activities in which they had been previously employed. Hence the term "sub-optimal employments" covers what we suggest,

4   in paragraph 4, is the most serious form of waste—the non-utilization of the *potential* capacity of the labor force in trades to which they have never been allowed to "become attached," but in which they could be fruitfully employed.

The magnitude of the waste hidden in sub-optimal employment may involve no "idleness" whatsoever. Both labor and the complementary assets which are labor's tools will eventually have become specialized to produce less-wanted kinds of things. Yet the prodigious waste will have no conspicuous, or even discernible (let alone measurable), manifestation in idleness. Suppose, for instance, in the United States inflation accelerates while minimum wage-rates are *not* raised to compensate. The deplorable idleness of juveniles will be mitigated or eliminated and the conspicuous injustices which, in 1976, are still visible in the demoralization of youth, particularly black youth, will be gradually eradicated. But the waste of human potentialities caused by strike-threat pressures and the enforcement of "the rate for the job principle"—the "equal pay for equal work principle"—will remain.[1]

South Africa provides a good example. The South African government has, in recent years, with shrewd political skill, been weakening time-honored barriers which until relatively recently had—on the grounds of protecting non-Whites from exploitation—confined them to sub-optimal tasks. The rate of progress of non-Whites has, however, been curbed somewhat, as the lowering of obstacles to equality of opportunity has occurred, by pressures upon the firms employing them to raise their wage-rates above the levels determined by rising demands for their services. The pressures have been thought expedient in order to appease uninformed or malicious critics abroad and at home, as well as to satisfy economically illiterate or sentimental humanitarians (among whom "liberal" parliamentarians, prominent businessmen and leading journalists are the least forgivable sinners). The belief that raising the wage-rates of the relatively poorer classes or races by edict or persuasion will enhance the aggregate earnings of that class must have retarded the escape of large sectors of the population from "sub-optimal" jobs. Racial injustices of historical origin toward those in chronic sub-optimal unemployments can be dissolved, however, through the eradication of customary or deliberate hindrances to the entry of all races into better remunerated and more productive work. And enforcement of "the rate for the job" remains, as we have seen (p. 129), the most powerful obstacle.

---

[1] The only effective way to achieve "equal pay for work of equivalent quality and quantity" is the creation of market freedom.

The last eight lines of paragraph 4 need further explanation. We have chosen a much better term for "diverted resources" (which we used in 1939), namely, "sub-optimal employment." But "sub-optimal employment" covers not only men and assets *forced out of* a field of employment but equally those *prevented from entering* it. What I meant to convey in the passage under discussion was that the "wasteful utilization" of men and assets discharged from a former occupation is much less important than the wasteful use of resources never having been allowed to enter privileged fields (meaning, by the latter, productive activities which would otherwise have constituted the most productive and best remunerated employment outlets). The important truth is that "sub-optimal employment" constitutes an incomparably greater burden on society than actual idleness in any of the categories we distinguish.

5   In paragraph 5 we have not made it sufficiently clear that, if marginal prospective yields to investment in replacement or net accumulation of a firm's assets stock decline, through enforced idleness or the withholding of capacity in respect of labor's inputs or other complementary inputs, the firm itself cannot be blamed for any shrinkage in, or curbed rate of growth in, its profitable output.

Chapter X

Withheld Capacity

1
"Withheld capacity" or "diverted resources" arise from voluntary monopolization

"Withheld capacity" arises when the State, or an individual or firm owning a "natural monopoly,"[1] or a firm uniting the ownership and control of competing resources, or a group of individuals or firms acting in collusion, cut down the output under their control with a view to securing the private benefits of contrived scarcities.[2] In so doing they obviously reduce the degree of utilization of the resources at their disposal in the particular productive process restrained. The phenomenon of "withheld capacity" will then exist if, for some other reason, the redundant resources are neither scrapped nor devoted (while specialized) to some alternative occupation. Resources which *do* find some other use are (as we have just pointed out) "diverted resources."

---

[1] On the distinction between "natural monopoly" and "natural scarcity" see HUTT, "Natural and Contrived Scarcities," *South African Journal of Economics,* September 1935. See also paragraph 19, below.

[2] In the case of the State, and when the resources are State-owned, taxation may be the motive.

They represent "waste" but there is no "idleness." Whenever a cartel reduces quotas or agrees to pay a bonus to a member in return for the nonutilization of the whole or some part of his plant, then the "withheld capacity" type of "participating idleness" will be brought about; or, if substitute utilization is resorted to, there will be "diverted resources"; or the "redundant" resources will be scrapped. Reductions of the working day with "work-sharing" motives are, as we have seen, a parallel in respect of labor.[3] "Withheld capacity" (like "enforced idleness") can only exist in isolation when it is left as "valueless resources" in respect of noncompeting utilization. It may then be said to be in its "pure" state. To be so regarded, equipment must have no positive net scrap value. If it is not in its "pure" state then it must be explained as being in "pseudo-idleness" *in respect of substitute employments,* or in "preferred idleness" (in the case of labor), or in "participating idleness."

2

Keynes' conceptions, "expectation
of return" and "disutility," cause the distinctions which
we have to discuss to be overlooked

*   Keynes' approach to the problem attempts to make complete abstraction of "withheld capacity" because of the notion of "expectation of return" which he regards as determining "the level of employment." If by "level of employment" is meant the degree of utilization of a given set of

---

[3] Of course, slow running in the case of plant and ca' canny in the case of labor may mean that there is no increase in the hours of conspicuous idleness. "Idling" may not be visibly recognizable as "idleness." But the problem is obviously similar. The "waste" is of the "idleness" type, not of the "diverted resources" type.

resources induced by a certain expectation of return in any industry, then it will be different according to the extent to which social institutions permit the autonomous or collusive contrivance of scarcities. Surely, then, the first stage of discussion should be focused on such institutions. The amount of natural resources or equipment offered employment in any industry of homogeneous production will be greater in the absence of a restrictive labor policy bearing on that industry; and the amount of employment of labor in such an industry will be greater in the absence of monopolistic arrangements among the owners of natural resources and equipment. Hence the study of idleness should concentrate on such restrictions, i.e., withholdings of capacity. In the actual world, the most effective collusion for restriction of production is that arranged jointly among cooperant as well as competing parties. In other words, capacity is widely withheld under "joint monopoly," rather than as a unilateral policy resulting in less "employment" being offered to the opposing parties. Apparently failing to see the significance of this, Keynes has unwittingly made "effective demand" depend on the productive power which the *entrepreneurs* who control productive power allow to be effective. "Effective demand," according to him, is the aggregate proceeds "which the *entrepreneurs* expect to receive, inclusive of the incomes which they will hand on to the other factors of production, from the amount of current employment which they decide to give."[4] His "effective demand" is, in short, consistent with, but just as useless as, his conception of "disutility" as "covering every kind of reason which might lead a man, or a body of men, to withhold their labor

---

[4] KEYNES, op. cit., p. 55.

rather than accept a wage which had to them a utility below a certain minimum."[5] And other writers have followed him in this sterile approach. Thus, Mr. R. F. Harrod takes as his "determinant," "any consideration relevant to the decision whether to do a given piece of work."[6] Unfortunately, "inducement to work" so defined not only places a screen round all the distinctions which this essay seeks to emphasize, but in particular diverts attention from the fact that considerations of private profit may induce a withholding of capacity for other reasons than the "utility" of leisure or the avoidance of "disutilities" other than the loss of monopoly revenue.

3

If the monopolists' optimum outputs
are everywhere attained before depression, the further
withholding of capacity in depression
cannot be simply explained

The motive to withhold capacity has a more complex significance than may appear at first. When the money demand for a product is falling, a privately serious distributive situation may develop for the owners of an enterprise. That is, their proportion of the receipts may fall. Now if an *entrepreneur* has throughout taken the maximum advantage of price and output agreements and has been charging the monopolists' optimum price for the product, he may be unable to resist a decline in the revenues of his firm by simply cutting output. A further restriction may not help him at all. For price depression must be in part expressed

---

[5] Ibid., p. 6.
[6] R. F. HARROD, *The Trade Cycle*, pp. 9–10.

through *entrepreneurs* in other lines of consumption under-cutting for the consumers' favor. Hence the demand sched-ule for his product is not only likely to fall but to present no less elasticity over the relevant compass. In other words, his optimum output may not fall at all when producers in supposedly noncompeting lines are observed to be compet-ing. Thus, a theater and cinema monopoly *may* find that it pays to lower charges for admission in times of depression to a level which results in approximately the same number of attendances. Given the obviously valid assumption that demand schedules are not independent of one another, there are no grounds for assuming that monopolists' opti-mum outputs will fall, on the whole, in times of what may be called "pure price depression."

4
A "pure" price depression does not
make the withholding of capacity more profitable

The discussion of this point nearly forces us into a field which we here wish to avoid, namely, the problem of "de-mand in general." But we draw no controversial conclu-sions. Let us assume that the "depression" is *purely* a price depression, with no initial withholding of capacity.[7] We can imagine the price depression to arise owing to an increased demand for an inelastic supply of money and money sub-stitutes. The effect of this will be that money incomes, i.e., the money valuation of the services of all resources, will fall. *Ceteris paribus,* the effect upon demand schedules will be a mere change of scale. E.g., in the simplest case of a

---

[7] That is, we assume that the quantity theory in its simplest form is opera-tive.

"costless" commodity the fall of demand can be represented as on the diagram below, in the shift from D_1 to D'_1. In spite of the fall, the optimum monopoly output remains at OQ_1, the optimum price changing from Q_1P_1 to $Q_1P'_1$. If it is argued that the *relative* demand for different types of services must necessarily be affected, then, if there is no withholding of capacity (and it is *this* phenomenon which we have to explain), some demand schedules will fall to, say, the position D_2 (i.e., a fall in relation to the new scale, so to speak) with the appropriate optimum outputs OQ_2. But others will rise to the position D_3, with appropriate outputs OQ_3. The aggregate effect seems likely to be neutral. The presence of contractual obligations, avoidable costs, and specificities does not affect this conclusion; outputs OQ_3

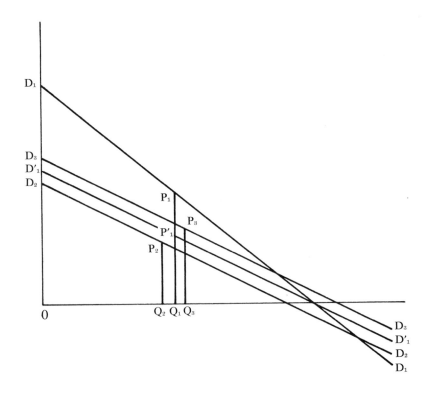

will be larger than they would otherwise be in consequence of specificities, and outputs OQ_3 smaller.[8]

5
Interloping is not less easy during pure price depression

It may be thought that the tendency toward monopolistic restriction of output is likely to be strengthened during price depressions by the reduced probability that interlopers will find it worth their while to construct new specialized equipment. Receipts may be well above *avoidable* costs for those who already own equipment, while they are below them for interlopers, who must incur the cost of new equipment before they can compete, and to whom, therefore, such cost is "avoidable." But this view assumes that the prices of the services which can make the equipment do not fall to an extent which makes interloping just as profitable. Only the withholding of such services would, in general, make interloping relatively unprofitable. The market value of existing equipment may maintain the same relative value to new equipment in times of price depression.

6
The withholding experienced in practice is due firstly to the relations of monopolistic cooperant producers

Why is it, then, that an increase of idleness is such a common response to trade depression? There appear to be two sets of reasons. The first arises out of the relations

*

---

[8] We cannot here discuss the supposed repercussions of the rise in the rate of interest upon the propensity to consume or to buy durable goods; for although it can be argued that a new preference for less physical consumption (e.g., of things other than leisure), or a new preference for more security (liquidity), can precipitate *valueless resources,* there are no grounds for assuming that they can lead to the further *withholding of capacity* in relation to the new preferences.

between cooperant producers who can share to some extent in monopoly revenues. If the whole chain of producers at all stages of the productive process were acting collusively[9] and rationally in response to the demand schedule for the final product, the considerations we discussed in paragraphs 3 to 5 would still apply. That output (or that price) determined by marginal receipts and marginal costs for the whole group would be to the advantage of the whole. (The division of the maximized net aggregate receipts is a subsidiary matter.) And in times of price depression, the optimum output would, *ceteris paribus,* be unchanged. But such perfectly collusive arrangements do not exist. Machinery for ideal collusion cannot be set up. Hence the maintenance of the price of the unfinished commodity at one stage, by one cooperant producer, may be to his advantage. The price he fixes does not affect, of course, that price for the final product which could produce the largest margin between aggregate receipts and expenses. But it *does* affect the avoidable expenses of each subsequent producer. This is simply because his claim on the value of what is finally sold is expressed in terms of price per unit.

7

The incentive, among cooperant monopolists, to arrange their collective optimum output is defeated in the scramble to preserve individual revenues

Unless there is some recognition of the collective private loss which is incurred in that way, and so the introduction of some collusive mitigation of the situation, the position

---

[9] We use the terms "collusive," "collusion," etc., with no suggestion of nefarious design, but in the sense of "cooperative," "cooperation." The latter terms would, unfortunately, have been even more misleading.

can arise that a further withholding of capacity is profitable
at each successive stage toward the final product. Such a
situation is more likely to be present, at any stage, the less
effective competition happens to be. The private disadvantageousness of the cumulative restriction from the point of
view of the whole chain of producers creates an incentive
toward the exercise of "reasonableness."[10] That is, there is
an incentive toward collusion with a view to mitigating the
results of general overrestrictionism, and if enlightenment
happens to accompany this incentive, agreements and bar-
gains resulting in the cutting of prices to consumers, and to
producers at successive stages, are likely to eventuate. Now
this will mean for each producer an output greater than that
indicated by marginal receipts and marginal expenses
before such agreements. The price fixed at any stage
through negotiation may result in the demand or the supply
schedule for the unfinished product rising. The extent to
which this is possible cannot itself be expressed in schedules. The output of each cooperant producer and the price
he obtains are as indeterminate as his share of the monopoly
revenues. It seems therefore that it is the absence of institutions to facilitate the required negotiations for the optimum
outputs which can cause the further withholding of capacity
in times of depression. A fall of prices can precipitate a new
scramble among cooperant monopolists to get as large a
proportion as possible of the aggregate monopoly revenues.
It may be set afoot by what are usually quite innocently
motivated attempts by each to maintain his former money
revenues. If the output of the final product had formerly
been the optimum for the whole chain, the new output will

---

[10] See below, Chap. XI, para. 1.

clearly be below it. From the social point of view, however, there are grounds for assuming that the further withholding is not so serious as this suggests. For it appears probable that the monopolists' optimum output is often exceeded in normal times.

8

The withholding is due secondly to outputs having previously exceeded the monopolists' optimum, probably owing to "reasonable" and not maximum profits having been sought

This brings us to the next conceivable explanation of the withholding of capacity in depression. It is possible that, in spite of the monopolistic organization of modern society, it would be wrong to suppose that the maximization of private profits is generally or frequently the goal of *entrepreneurs;* or, if it is, in a vague way, the object of their policy, that they are fairly unsuccessful in attaining their aim. What seems to happen is that most often the aim of producers enjoying a monopoly position is that of earning "reasonable" not maximum profits. The typical output under monopolistic conditions is above the monopolists' short-run optimum and quite frequently above the long-run optimum. Whether this is due to a fear of the consequences of public indignation, or to a fear of giving undue encouragement to interlopers, or to a sincere feeling of responsibility toward consumers, or to a belief that a price only slightly higher than that which has ruled in the past is obviously "fair," the fact seems to be that few firms have really conceived of the notion of the monopolists' optimum price, still less have they tried to seek it. Even in cost accounting the conception has never intruded, and until economic analysis has some impact upon the minds of business men and accountants, it will hardly affect conscious policy. Moreover, under what has been called the "tacit monopoly" or "oligopoly" relationship, the same holds true. In these circumstances, the apparently competing firms are pursuing the policy which is loosely described by the words "live and let live." They act "reasonably" by refraining from price cutting, in the knowledge that they would all suffer if they did start cutting prices. Such a situation is probably nothing more than the result of the rather passive, uncritical acceptance of a customary and therefore supposedly "reasonable" price. The monopolists' optimum price of the product for the group as a whole under tacit collusion is, in the abstract, as determinate as under formal monopoly. But in the actual world that we know, the *entrepreneurs* concerned can hardly be regarded as groping to find it. All they want is "fair" prices, "remunerative" prices, prices which will enable their profits to expand in accordance with their "reasonable" expectations. Hence actual prices in those circumstances must often fall much below the short-run optimum and probably below the long-run optimum also; and when depression comes the *entrepreneurs* find that they are in a position to minimize their losses by withholding capacity.

9
A group may withhold capacity in its short-run interest, and against its long-run interest

But even when the withholding of capacity which most effectively protects the earning power of a producing group in the short-run is contrary to the long-run interests of those in it, the policy is still likely to be practiced. For in times of depression, *entrepreneurs* may often be dominated by the *short-run* situation. In respect of policy determined by company directors anticipating angry meetings of share-holders, this is very likely. For reasons such as these, there-fore, an almost universal phenomenon of trade depression is the widespread attempt "not to spoil the market" (as the phrase goes), or to retain "fair" and "remunerative" prices.[11] Those policies are nearly always thought of in terms of the securing of prosperity. But it is obvious that "prosperity" in those terms spells "waste," and the "waste" may be mani-fested in "idleness."

10

Irrational withholding of capacity is
particularly likely owing to the practical indeterminateness
of the monopolists' optimum

*   Such irrational withholding by monopolists is particularly likely for another practical reason. Even if we imagine that

---

[11] As a rule, the notion of "not spoiling the market" is hardly a rational one; it usually implies nothing more definite than is conveyed by the phrase "cut-throat competition." But it may have a more definite meaning. This arises from the belief that a temporary fall in price may result in an increased elasticity of demand for a product at prices above that to which it falls. Such a phenomenon would be explicable on the grounds that purchasers get used to the lower price, come to regard it as just or as the correct price, adjust their other expenditure to it, and in further ways come to acquire an outlook which leads them to spend relatively less in buying the commodity when it returns to its former price. The loss in such a case is a private one, however. We must remain neutral on the question of the goodness of such a situation. But if, as the effect of the temporary fall, taste and preference are materially and widely altered, it may be interpreted as a desirable thing. We can regard it as having stimulated an experiment in the distribution of individual spending power leading to a deliberate change in that distribu-tion. The fear of spoiling the market must be distinguished from the fear of causing the monopoly to break by price cutting.

the notion of the monopolists' optimum is vaguely or clearly understood by those *entrepreneurs* who are confronted with circumstances which can make restriction of output profitable; even if we assume that such *entrepreneurs* have some grasp of the connected notions of marginal receipts and marginal costs (which define the optimum); it does not appear probable that the long-run optimum will be located except in the roughest possible manner. In practice, the aim of maximizing profits must be pursued through halting experimental price changes. And *entrepreneurs'* price strategy must be formulated in the knowledge that the short-run reactions will give a most uncertain indication of ultimate results. Furthermore, the trial and error of *immediate* policy must itself determine in part what the most profitable *eventual* price should be, through its repercussions upon tastes, consumers' views about price reasonableness, and interloping and substitutional development. This being so, it seems probable that although the long-run maximization of profits may on occasion be an ideal which is sought as rationally as is practically conceivable, the actual position will be but vaguely determinable by *entrepreneurs*. Hence a strong temptation to follow short-run policies may be expected to arise in times of difficulty. That is, it is especially probable that in a proportion of cases the further withholding of capacity will appear to be the most likely means of easing *private* (e.g., from the point of view of a firm) distributive difficulties. Trade depression is therefore liable to be met by the maintenance (or only slight lowering) of prices which have seemed "fair" and "reasonable." This is possibly a very important cause of price and wage-rate inertia in certain monopolized industries, and so of the withholding of capacity during trade depression in those industries.

11

Withheld capacity may be *"individually rational" but "collectively irrational"*

*   Now it is obvious that, whether privately justified or not, the "withholding of capacity" can never be to the advantage of all producing groups, considered collectively, if they all pursue the policy. That is, it cannot benefit society.[12] On the other hand, it may well benefit some groups considered individually, if they can follow it and the producers of other things (for which they are consumers) are unable to do so. Hence, it may be individually rational while collectively irrational. But the policy of one group which simply refrains from restriction cannot thereby *force* other groups to abandon their restrictive policies. Only collective action through the State can prevent the holding back of productive power in the private interest.

---

[12] It might be urged in criticism of this sort of assertion that it is based on an analysis which ignores the financial consequences of value changes. In the world as it actually is, the withholding of capacity might be held to be socially beneficial if used to obviate bankruptcies, insolvencies, forced sales and recapitalizations with all their disturbing effects upon financial markets. But all sorts of otherwise indefensible policies could be defended on similar grounds, namely, that they preserve a distributive situation due to faulty capitalization policy in the past from violent change and from consequent destructive repercussions. How far it is justifiable to ignore the long-run effects of protecting *entrepreneurs* from the consequences of their own erroneous actions we cannot here discuss; for we are not attempting to deal with the expediencies which must dominate practical policies. We are simply concerned to make clear all the issues which should be considered in the formulation of policies.

12
Withheld capacity may be
"individually rational" and irrational for the group

Moreover, as we have seen in paragraphs 6 and 7, in respect of the relations between producers in the different cooperant stages of production a similar situation can exist. The producers at one stage cannot *force* those at other stages to drop restrictive policies by merely themselves refraining from restricting. To evade such a monopoly, they must find (or be known to be in a position to find) interlopers who may be induced to break into the monopolized cooperant field of production. But private or State powers of coercion frequently make this impossible. It follows that, in times of depression, and under States which encourage or tolerate restrictionism, the maintenance of prices (i.e., the withholding of capacity) is often the most advantageous response from the private point of view. And the output for the industry may frequently be brought, therefore, *below* the optimum for the industry as a whole. In such cases the withholding may be said to be "individually rational" but irrational for the group. "Reasonableness" alone will enable withheld capacity to be reutilized and the optimum for the industry as a whole to be reached, unless collective action through the State dissolves all restrictions.

13
When indivisibilities are large,
the withholding of capacity may not, in rare circumstances,
conflict with the consumers' sovereignty ideal

In one set of circumstances, the withholding of capacity

by an individual *entrepreneur* has some apparent justification in the light of the consumers' sovereignty ideal, namely,
in all those cases in which price discrimination by a natural
monopolist is to any extent defensible. Such cases are, we
believe, of negligible importance in practice;[13] but for completeness we must mention them here. For simplicity, let us
consider the situation in the absence of price discrimination.
The problem arises owing to what has been called the
"technical factor," the indivisibility of the efficient unit of
supply of certain kinds of equipment. For example, a machine capable of producing 100 units of service a day may
be purchased, while only 50 units of service are actually
required, the reason being that a smaller machine is unobtainable at all, or unobtainable except at a higher cost.
Hence, with a constant demand, there will be some continuous "surplus capacity." If this "surplus capacity" has no
hire value, it merely represents pseudo-idleness. If it *has*
hire value, it appears at first to represent withheld capacity.
But if competitors actually *had* the right to bid for its unutilized services in that case, they might be able to undercut
the original *entrepreneur*. The "full employment" of that
plant, if the sense defined in Chapter 1 is crudely interpreted, might result in its capital value falling to less than
was originally paid for it. It is theoretically possible, therefore, that only the ability to prevent interlopers from using
that capacity in such cases would lead to the enterprise
being undertaken at all. Under existing institutions, of
course, natural monopoly already gives more than sufficient
protection when this situation is in any measure present;

---

[13] See on this point HUTT, "Discriminating Monopoly and the Consumer,"
Economic Journal, March 1936.

and under competitive institutions, a limited right to "withhold capacity," if that term is really justified in this sort of
case, could be conferred on an *entrepreneur* by contract
prior to investment, when clear-cut indivisibilities acting in
the manner here described could be proved. In such a case,
the contractually permitted idleness ought to be regarded as
pseudo-idleness, just as a patent restriction which is really
in the consumers' interest ought not to be regarded as leading to a contrived scarcity in the light of the consumers'
sovereignty ideal. There is really "full employment" of a
piece of equipment in our sense if those who voluntarily
make use of its product are called upon to pay a sum the
expectation of which is the minimum required to make its
provision profitable.[14]

14

*Keynes' "involuntary unemployment" may be
intended to refer to the case of withheld labor capacity
which is "collectively irrational"*

We can now return to Keynes' conception of "invol-   *
untary" unemployment. In Chapter VI, we pointed out that
the workers' alleged resistance to wage-rate reductions and

---

[14] If price discrimination is practiced, in the circumstances which justify
that practice, full (i.e., optimum) employment may exist in spite of
capacity being *apparently withheld* from those purchasers from whom the
higher price is demanded, and in spite of that capacity being *apparently*
left as "diverted resources" (i.e., utilized for the benefit of those purchasers
from whom the lower prices are demanded). But defensible discrimination
(or the parallel withholding of capacity under uniform charging) is really
nothing more than a means of enabling those classes of consumers for
whom certain goods or services satisfy relatively urgent wants to induce
entrepreneurs to invest the necessary capital. Discrimination enables the
entrepreneur to recoup himself for such capital expenditure from the consumers who pay the higher price. After a while, that capital must be re-

their alleged acquiescence in a rise in the cost of living might not be due to "irrational preferences." Such a situation *could* be due, instead, to irrational policies, which is an entirely different question. It is obvious from our discussion in paragraphs 11–12 that there is no essential irrationality in respect of restrictive or exclusive policies *judged by standards of private advantage.* But there may be gross blindness in the failure to work for the collective removal of restrictions and exclusions which may be collectively burdensome to all; and other practical circumstances may lead to misconceived policies. We agree with Keynes (if this is his suggestion) that grave misconceptions frequently bear on policy in the field of labor whenever the workers endorse, or their leaders formulate, policies which withhold or exclude labor. The collective aspect of restrictionism may not be seen and the workers may be injured by their intended protections. In endeavoring to obtain the maximum earnings for themselves their attention may be focused on money rates. What earnings can purchase for the recipients may be but dimly envisaged as a connected result. And the "cost" relationship of one industry to another may be equally vaguely perceived. If the leaders of organized labor really understood how private restrictionism burdened the laboring classes as a whole, they might recommend wage-rate reductions to prevent a futile, self-stimulating and cumulative withholding of capacity. But widespread reciprocal action, involving also the mitigation of restrictions imposed in the defense of dividends, might be necessary to make such a policy seem superficially tolerable.

---

garded as paid off, however; and then continued idleness *may* entail real withholding of capacity, and continued discrimination *must* entail real withholding of capacity and diversion of resources.

15

*Keynes' conception seems to be based on
the assumption that the power to withhold capacity
cannot be restrained and that the resulting idleness can
be avoided only through monetary policies*

The "involuntary unemployment" which Keynes dis-   *
cusses may possibly be meant, then, to refer to "collective
irrationalities" in the sense which we have just discussed. If
so, he seems to be arguing that restrictionism in the labor
market constitutes an insurmountable barrier, and that re-
adjustments eliminating "involuntary unemployment" can
be obtained only through the "real" rates of earnings of
labor being reduced in a *tactful* way, i.e., by leaving money
wage rates untouched, a stratagem which can be best accomplished by inflating prices through monetary policy. Unless
this is a misinterpretation of his view, he cannot rightly
compare orthodox economists (who hold that restrictionism—whether rational or irrational—cannot be taken for
granted) with "Euclidean geometers in a non-Euclidean
world, who discovering that in experience straight lines
apparently parallel often meet, rebuke the lines for not
keeping straight."[15] Those orthodox writers who have sought
to apply classical theory to social problems have thought in
terms of institutions, human knowledge and the observed
conduct of men. Experience of these things has never led to
their being *expressly* described as inevitable by the critics of
orthodoxy. How far can the social scientist so regard them?
Suppose the source of rigidity in the labor market has to be
ascribed to the necessity for saving the face and preserving

---

[15] KEYNES, op. cit., p. 16.

the livelihood of trade union leaders; or suppose it is believed to be due to the fact that the finance of a large political party and the maintenance by it of an immediately
purposeful and popular program necessitates the continued
belief on the part of the masses that wage cuts represent the
exploitation of the "have-nots" by the "haves"; or suppose
we feel that the origin of such rigidity lies deeper and involves capital organization and ideologies as much as it
does those of labor; are we, as practical economists or
sociologists, to accept these facts as natural or as inevitable
and so treat them as fundamental assumptions?

16
The economist cannot regard
the withholding of capacity as inevitable

*   The politicians may have to regard certain irrational monopolistic policies as inevitable during the present age. And
as pure theorists, we may find it convenient, on occasion,
to reason from the assumption that a rigidity based on palpable social blindness is unavoidable. If so, we must state
that assumption explicitly. But as realistic students of society, we have to face the truth that such rigidities are based
on institutions which it appears to be within the power of
society to change. The politicians may well retort that to
be frank about this issue is to display a pathetic political
naïveté; that to question the sanctity of the right of "collective bargaining" must of necessity condemn the social scientist to impotence. But that can hardly deter those of us
who are not selling policies in return for power. We need
not, indeed we must not, accept the view that because the
leaders of labor will not advise a strike for increased wage
rates against a rising cost of living, while they will be forced

to resist wage cuts, an inflationary policy is justified in the light of some accepted social ideal. As realistic students of contemporary institutions, are we not bound to recognize the stark fact that the system whose effects it is hoped to avoid by the inflation stratagem remains unshaken? Of course, Mr. Keynes' case for the monetary policies he recommends rests upon much more subtle arguments than those which we have here examined; and he would certainly deny that his suggestions can rightly be called "inflationary." But it does appear to be crude reasoning of this type which is most likely to win for his point of view the support of "practical men."

17
On the concepts of "collusive" and "natural" monopolies

In this discussion, we have used the term "monopolist" to   *
cover controllers of natural monopolies as well as controllers of collusive monopolies. A monopoly is "natural" when it does not depend upon any amalgamation of interests through the purchase of competing resources or any other form of contractual or tacit collusion. In practice, the natural monopolist is one who owns some unique source of supply, or enjoys what the present writer has called "the advantage of site and size" (i.e., "geographical advantage" or "scale of production advantage"). Now, every *entrepreneur* confronted with a downward sloping long-run demand schedule is a monopolist unless his autonomy is limited in some other way. And one method of attempting to limit such autonomy in the case of natural monopoly is public utility control. The object of public utility control is presumably to restrict *entrepreneurial* powers in such a way as to convert a monopolistic situation into a competitive one.

We use the term "competitive" because the attempt is clearly to enable the disposal of the resources at the *entrepreneur's* command, not according to private interest, but in accordance with the interests of society; and the free movement and utilization of resources, regardless of private interests which are thereby injured, is what orthodox economists have in fact meant by competition. That was, by implication, the traditional meaning of the term until recent abstract expositions started applying adjectives like "monopolistic," "imperfect" or "impure" to "competition." Distinctive names may be more appropriately applied to the institutions within which the essentially homogeneous force of competition tends to bring about an equilibrium. One does not talk about "buoyant," "imperfect" or "impure" gravity because there are balloons and aeroplanes.

18

The abuse of natural monopoly requires restriction of entry, just as under collusive monopoly

*   The natural monopolist is in a position to benefit by allowing scarce resources or scarce available services to be wasted; and he is in a position also to exclude resources from coming in to cooperate in the field under his control. That is, he can limit investment to his own advantage. But he is in that position because of existing institutions. Hence Mr. Kaldor's suggestion[16] that the notion of "institutional" monopolies should be confined to those based on "restriction of entry," and that natural monopolies (arising from economies of scale) should cease to be termed "monopolies" seems to be based upon misconceptions. Natural monop-

---

[16] *Quarterly Journal of Economics,* May 1938, pp. 523–29.

olies equally exist because institutions permit them. And they restrict "freedom of entry" in exactly the same way that collusive monopolies do. This is most clear in respect of the amount of *cooperant* resources which they allow in. Their demand for such resources is limited by the identical principles which limit collusive monopolists' demand for cooperant resources. But even when they waste part of the supply of "costless" but scarce homogeneous products (e.g., a mineral water spring, part of whose output is allowed to run to waste), they do so by "restricting entry" in the sense that they deny access to the supply. And when natural monopolists "withhold capacity," they do so for the same reasons as collusive monopolists, and with the same effects.

19
Apart from the case of large public utilities,
natural monopoly is of relatively small importance

We have thought it necessary to make this point because there seems to be a rather vague tendency in some academic quarters to suggest that, because natural monopoly exists, and because to some extent almost all productive activities enjoy some uniqueness, attempts to create competitive institutions must be visionary. Such a view implies that withheld capacity is inevitable when it depends upon natural monopoly. We do not accept that view, although we cannot here discuss the institutions necessary to limit the autonomy of natural monopolies, just as we have not here been concerned with the actual means of dissolving collusive monopolies. But we admit that the problem of public utility control has so far received even less satisfactory discussion than the problem of antitrust policy in respect of amalgamations and associations. And it may well be that control of the former constitutes a much more practically difficult problem than control of the latter. Nevertheless, the framers of social policy who are concerned with the idleness of resources and its connected problems need not be unduly perturbed by such difficulties. For apart from the large public utilities (which are in any case usually protected also by collusive agreements or legal enactment), natural monopoly can be observed in practice to be of relatively small importance *in comparison with collusive monopoly*. In the absence of collusive monopoly (in conspicuous or unrecognized form) there can be little withholding of capacity.[17] It is true that each individual in the labor market may, in addition to purchasing leisure, endeavor to maximize his earnings by holding back his services. But only in the case of rare skills, such as those of virtuoso musical performers, can any importance be attached to this possibility.

---

[17] The reader must be reminded that the withholding of stocks has nothing to do with the withholding of capacity. Stocks of commodities are only withheld in our sense when their liquidation is proceeding at a rate slower than that required by the social interest (that is, under the consumers' sovereignty criterion, consumers' interest). See Chap. III, para. 13.

Appendix

Notes and Comments on Chapter X

An important point that we fail to make sufficiently explicit in Chapter X is that while "enforced idleness" and "withheld capacity" both involve the *waste* of assets and human talents (even when they take the form of a temporary condition of "participating idleness," or when they are in the process of transition into "sub-optimal employment"), *the waste is chiefly expressed, not simply as the nonuse or underuse of the resources themselves but as induced idleness in certain noncompeting resources.*[1] Through the extermination of potential inputs in any one productive activity, there must be (in the light of Say's law) an eradication of a source of demands for certain noncompeting outputs and inputs.

"Real recession" (as distinct from what we have called *"price* recession") is nothing more than the contagious spread of wasteful idleness; and *ceteris paribus* the idleness

---

[1] The reason why, in 1939, we did not touch on this important issue was that (as is explained in para. 4, and in the original and second prefaces) we wanted to avoid "the problem of 'demand in general.' "

caused by each mispricing spreads because there is always *some* measure of price rigidity in noncompeting activities. Economic coordination requires both price and quantity adjustments; and (partly because all decision-makers are fallible) every particular case of "enforced idleness" or "withheld capacity" tends to precipitate another, with a consequential cumulative shrinkage of real income.

An important psychological factor has to be reckoned with. An immediate incentive for induced mispricing is entrepreneurial disappointments due to changes in the composition of the assets stock which turn out to have been wasteful. For reasons which the Austrian economists (in particular, Hayek) have stressed, attempts to use credit expansion to mitigate the income-depressing consequences of inputs and outputs priced above market-clearing levels aggravate the disorder. The information-communication function of the pricing system is upset. False market signals are emitted in the form of low market rates of interest caused, not by a normal rise in people's desire to provide for the future, but simply through an increase in money-spending power via bank advances. In the author's own terminology, this leads to an unduly high proportion of assets of relatively long prospective or intended life span (i.e., producer goods) in the aggregate assets stock, and hence an unduly low proportion of assets of relatively short prospective or intended life span (i.e., consumer goods). Such a distortion of the assets structure ultimately brings about *general* disappointment of entrepreneurial expectations.[2] Demands as a whole turn out to be lower than had been counted on. Pessimism displaces optimism. Prospective

---

[2] Moreover, the arbitrariness of government controls enhances the likelihood of disappointments because of erroneous predictions.

yields shrink and hence investments in inputs shrink. The deterioration may be aggravated because nearly all corporation managements, acting entrepreneurially, are "price searchers," confronted with downward-sloping short-run demand curves. Such managements, for reasons we have noticed (pp. 202–4), may have been pricing their outputs well under the short-term profit-maximizing level. When sales fall off, such price searchers seem often to respond (acting as much in the *intended* interests of the majority of their employees as in the interests of their stockholders) by failing to reduce the prices of their outputs to the lower market-clearing values established, a reaction which may well, *in the short run,* minimize any decline in their *pecuniary* earnings. Such reactions may be the result of predictions of an early recovery of demand, in which case entrepreneurs are *investing* in the accumulating inventories, and their output prices may not exceed market-clearing levels. Otherwise, if rational, they will invest in a reduced value of inputs.

Entrepreneurs may of course try (an almost impossible task) to persuade their employees to reduce the costs of labor inputs to values compatible with profitable full employment for their employees. That would tend to raise prospective yields, as a whole, and help maintain outputs and the contribution of the outputs to the source of demands. But as we have seen, every shrinkage of an output tends to activate a *cumulative* withholding of productive capacity. In such a situation governments have a vital function. But they are typically reluctant to exercise the kind of leadership required: namely, to encourage the downward cost adjustments which could restore the full flow of wages and income. In practice, therefore, once such a situation results, it typically deteriorates. Before long, drastic adjustments become essential for noninflationary recovery. But when self-aggravating mispricing of this type is recognized as to blame for recession, it must not be inferred that the pricing system has failed. Government has failed to perform its "classical" task of preventing one person or corporation from harming ("exploiting") another.[3]

Reliance upon credit expansion instead of price adjustment to recoordinate a disordered economy can be diagnosed, then, as the root cause of depression. Nevertheless, rectification is always *economically* possible, even if not *politically* possible,[4] without the greater harm of inflation, and at little cost if the required steps are taken early, but at continuously rising costs as the situation deteriorates. The belief that pricing to suit private or sectional interests (via government protections or otherwise) is an effective means of restoring prosperity in depression has been a disastrous illusion.

---

[3] Under J. S. Mill's criterion of defensible governmental action, which is to protect each person from being harmed by another, the prevention of "exploitation" is essential in a market economy. We have defined exploitation as:

> Any action taken, whether or not through discernible private coercion (collusion) or governmental coercion, or whether through monopolistic or monopsonistic power, which, under a given availability of resources (including the stock of knowledge and skills), reduces the value of the property or income of another person or group of persons, or prevents that value from rising as rapidly as it otherwise would, *unless this effect is brought about through* (a) the dissolution of some monopolistic or monopsonistic privilege; or (b) the substitution of some cheaper method (labor- or capital-saving) of achieving any objective (including the production and marketing of any output); or (c) the expression of a change in consumers' preference; or (d) taxation authorized by explicit legislation accepted as legitimate in any context. (HUTT, *Say's Law*, p. 23.)

[4] See W. H. HUTT, *Politically Impossible* . . .? Institute of Economic Affairs, London, 1971.

The practical path to any full employment and depression-avoidance policy will have to be by a refashioning of the legal framework of the economic system (via constitutional enactments) so that neither the legislature nor the executive shall have the right to restrain productivity or the market on behalf of private interests; while private interests shall also be denied the right to enrich themselves directly through the impoverishment of others (as, for example, through use of coercive practices like strikes, boycotts, etc.). For restraints on production and trade are depressants. They reduce the source of uninflated demands —"real income." Whether this truth could be communicated effectively to opinion-makers is not our present concern.

The required constitutional framework would have to aim at releasing and protecting entrepreneurial incentives for (a) the substitution of prospectively lower-cost methods of producing and marketing any product, and (b) the substitution of any prospectively preferred product. And these incentives are "the loss-avoidance, profit-seeking incentives" confronted with prospective yields from different "assets mixes" and different "input mixes" on the profitability of which entrepreneurs (ultimately investors) are prepared to assume the risk. No better arrangement has ever been suggested for minimizing the emergence or persistence of wasteful idleness or wasteful use of resources under "democratic consumers' sovereignty."[5]

---

[5] "Consumers' sovereignty" may be said to be "democratic" when every person's vote in the the market (through buying or refraining from buying final services or products offered) is weighted in proportion to the market value of the contribution of his services and those of his assets to the common pool of inputs.

2   Our argument in paragraph 2 is relevant to the original
publisher's claim on the cover jacket, which Lindley Fraser
denied (see the Preface to this 2nd edition), namely, "that
the book is largely devoted to criticism of Mr. Keynes'
General Theory." For, although we do not, in the 1939 text,
deal directly with the issues discussed in this appendix, we
do claim explicitly that Keynes placed "a screen around all
the distinctions which this essay seeks to emphasize." We
show, indeed, that Keynes' "effective demand" is, in his
words, made to "depend on the productive power which the
entrepreneurs who control productive power allow to be effective," while his conception of the incentives to withhold
productive power is made to cover "every kind of reason
which might lead a man or a body of men *to withhold their
labor* rather than accept a wage rate which had to them a
utility below a certain minimum" (our italics). Keynes'
blindness (and that of his apostles) lay in his failure to
perceive that *all* withholdings of supplies, and not only of
labor's inputs, were withholdings of demands for noncompeting inputs and outputs. Our 1939 reasoning (in para-
2   graph 2) does, we believe, bring into focus what the whole
of this work has been trying *inter alia* to explain, namely,
the serious inadequacy of some of the crucial concepts of
the Keynesian thesis. Sympathetically interpreted, our argument can be seen to tie up logically with our later criticisms
of the crucial notions of Keynes' *General Theory.*[6]
4   We must emphasize that, in paragraph 4, not only is
"costless production" assumed but also what we have termed
"pure price depression." It must be admitted that both
assumptions are highly notional, abstractly conceived con-

---

[6] *Keynesianism* and *Say's Law.*

ditions. Prices generally are supposed to have fallen, but not outputs. Our intention in using such abstractions is to clarify exposition. But today we no longer judge that the method is really helpful in this case. Even so, some economists might still differ with our present judgment.

Our references in paragraph 6 to "marginal costs" and 6 "marginal receipts" as determinants of prices and inputs ought to have been qualified by the adjective "prospective." But although, in previous publications, we ourselves had insisted on the importance of expectations in all entrepreneurial decision-making, we had not, in 1939, absorbed the full implications of the Austrian approach. We *had* certainly been influenced by Hayek's 1935 article on the maintenance of capital intact;[7] but it was only after the publication in English of Mises' *Human Action,* that we realized how important it was to remind the reader constantly that the prices or values on which all rational entrepreneurial decisions are based are *forecast* prices or values—extrapolations of current prices and values.

The distinction in paragraph 10 between *immediate* 10 pricing policy and *long-run* pricing policy is not quite satisfactory because it does not adequately treat the case of the competing firm which is nevertheless a "price searcher," being confronted with a downward-sloping demand curve for its output. In the original text a monopolist with true exploitative power is postulated. But everything we have remarked about this case applies equally (and more realistically) to the firm which, although having some discretion in respect of prices and output magnitudes, has no ability to profit from exploitation. The managers of such a firm

---

[7] F. A. HAYEK, "The Maintenance of Capital," *Economica,* August 1935.

may have little confidence in their initial judgment that the outputs they provide, and hence the prices they can profitably charge will in fact maximize realized yields. But they do know that if they price their outputs too high, they may benefit therefrom in the short run. In the long run, however, they will divert customers to other suppliers and generally stimulate growth on the part of their known and unknown competitors. Rivals will, they may fear, even invest in additional equipment (say of nonversatile machinery sunk into concrete), develop their customers' good-will, build up their salesmen's contacts with customers and acquire general knowledge of the market. All these consequences are threatened should they happen to overcharge. Moreover, it is not only competitors in the same line of production of whom they are afraid. Interindustry competition is a factor which cannot be ignored. This is especially so when competition has been expressed through those economies of scale which have (on occasion enormously) reduced operating costs and marketing margins for consumers' benefit. The *probability* in such circumstances is that product prices will be fixed initially well *below* those which would have resulted in the greatest yields in the long run. Unless our thinking here is defective, the mere fact that most manufacturing firms are confronted with downward-sloping demand curves does not imply that, in the *absence of deliberate collusion,* they would be in a position to withhold capacity or, by some device, enforce idleness in capacity for their private benefit.

11, 12   We have stated, in both paragraphs 11 and 12, that "only collective action through the State can prevent the holding back of productive power in the private interest." But that word "only" suggests, quite wrongly, that monopolies can never disintegrate through internal divergencies of interest.

Nevertheless, despite weighty arguments against antitrust which libertarian economists have been advancing in recent years, we adhere to the conclusion that a legal framework to create or protect incentives to substitute lower cost methods or preferred products is a necessary condition for market freedom to exist. This does not imply, however, that antitrust *in its present form* cannot be validly judged as more deleterious than nonintervention.

The consequences of collusive monopoly or natural monopoly abuses may be less burdensome than the system that has ruled in the United States since the late 1930s. In our present judgment, virtually all observable cases of apparent abuse of monopolistic power outside the labor market arise, in the present age, through legislation *intended* to prevent competition, or through the private use of coercive power, tolerated by legislators, in the form of the strike-threat (whether or not that threat is supplemented by the threat to boycott, to incite sabotage or to resort to violence). We believe that the effective application of antitrust to labor would eliminate some of the worst abuses of monopolistic power *outside* (*as well as inside*) *the labor market*. In particular it could reduce the burdens of "joint monopoly" in "sweetheart contracts," through which the legal right of a union to exploit consumers is used to validate what would be (in the United States) a criminal act on the part of corporations if committed without union collaboration.

But the universalization of antitrust in its present form might not be sufficient to ensure that privately engineered attempts at monopolization would all fail, through the internal strains which, in practice, often undoubtedly do cause cartel arrangements (or less formal price agreements) to disintegrate.

After more than 45 years of thinking about this problem, the author has reached the conclusion that the crucial weakness of the U.S. antitrust law, and other legislation with similar intent, is that they have made "monopoly," or the attempt to create "monopoly," the offense to be penalized. What the original antitrust reformers were really aiming at, however, was the "contrived scarcity" or, in the case of *monopsony,* the "contrived plenitude."[8] What *could* usefully be declared unlawful under antitrust are practices and procedures which cause certain things to be scarce which would otherwise be plentiful. And surely *this* is a relatively easily achievable objective. Excluding the cases of *natural* monopoly or *natural* monopsony, it can be seen that in every case of the successful contrivance of scarcity or the contrivance of plenitude, the services of assets or men can be perceived to have been *excluded from* some area, industry, firm or occupation; or (the monopsony case) having been *confined to* an area, industry, firm or occupation. Have we not here a concrete notion that lawyers and judges would be able to understand? And would not the "shutting in" or "shutting out" of capital or labor nearly always be conspicuous?

In the case of natural monopolies, the problem is not so simple. In principle there is a case for collective control. But when we consider actual experience of control of public utility rates, it is difficult to approve of the system in operation. For instance, in the United States we judge that electricity, gas and transport charges are nearly everywhere *very much higher* than they would have been in the long run had the maximization of prospective yields to investors been

---

[8] See W. H. HUTT, "Natural and Contrived Scarcities," *South African Journal of Economics,* September 1935.

permitted. But that is mainly because the politicians have got their hands into the process. It is all too easy for them to seek popularity by shouting everywhere that public utility charges are too high, or, under inflation, to cry that the upward adjustment of prices that the utilities request are unreasonable attempts to gouge consumers. Such politicians exploit the ignorance of electorates who seldom understand that, in reducing the prospective profitability of replacing or adding to the capital employed, they are often frustrating the achievement of formidable economies. When the charges permitted are determined largely in the light of their immediate popularity with the voters, how can we expect investment to be attracted into the capital- or labor-economizing nonversatile plant and equipment needed?[9]

But destruction of antimonopoly purpose through the vote-gathering pressures of politics is not confined to controls on public utilities. The antitrust laws of the United States have obviously been used to intimidate the managements of large corporations. It is widely suspected, in the United States, for instance, that corporations which try meticulously to obey the law and the spirit of the law, but do not contribute to "campaign expenses," or contribute to the wrong party, or in any other way offend governments, can be threatened with the enormous costs of defending antitrust suits. And when such suits are brought, the corporations find themselves confronted with the often-exposed absurdity that if a large corporation reduces its prices, that can be interpreted as predatory selling (see Chapter XI),

---

[9] In an inflation, the socially harmful consequences are magnified. The costs of replacement of worn-out equipment increase rapidly, while attempts by the utilities to value presently owned equipment at its full replacement value are condemned.

i.e., as an attempt to eliminate competitors and achieve a monopoly; and if it conforms to the prices charged by its rivals, that will be proof that it is participating in a collusive monopoly; while if it raises its prices, that is a proof of the exploitation of consumers through an abuse of monopolistic power.

13   The discussion in paragraph 13 of price discrimination, which we describe as a point of "negligible importance in practice," needs some further explanation. Price discrimination to different classes of purchasers is *possible* only under the discretion enjoyed by a "price searcher," i.e., an entrepreneur confronted with a downward-sloping demand curve. The assumption (in paragraph 13) is that such discrimination will be socially advantageous when the parties discriminated against are *beneficiaries* therefrom. Then, if the maintenance of prices against the latter is deemed profitable when demand for the product declines, but a recovery of demand is forecast, any idle capacity in fixed assets which results may be in pseudo-idleness rather than withheld capacity.

The reasons for the qualification in the last four lines of footnote 14 are of a pragmatic nature. They are explained in our 1936 article, already mentioned in footnote 13.

14   The reader should be reminded that paragraph 14 was written at a time when Britain had no statute law to restrain monopolistic abuse, while the ancient common law against "restraint of trade," which, in our judgment, could have been quite effective, had been virtually destroyed through court decisions by judges who were almost illiterate in the field of economics.[10]

---

[10] See W. H. HUTT, *Plan for Reconstruction*, Kegan Paul, London, 1943, pp. 223–26.

We returned, in our book, *Politically Impossible . . .?*,[11] to the problems raised in paragraphs 15 and 16. There we reasserted that the rigidities which Keynes assumed in the passage just quoted (in paragraph 15) implied the assumption of "palpable social blindness." Moreover, our argument in *Politically Impossible . . .?* develops the point (made in paragraph 16) that if such assumptions *are* made, they ought to be explicit. But the assumptions of wage-rate rigidity in the *General Theory* are obscured in the passages to which we were referring in our admission (in paragraph 16) that Keynes' case "rests upon much more subtle arguments than those which we have here examined." This is a reference to Keynes' argument which intended to explain the possibility of "unemployment equilibrium," a notion which no longer has any serious defenders, although it has been allowed to survive in many textbooks.

15, 16

15

16

16

Our judgment about the importance of natural monopoly (reflected in paragraphs 17 to 19) has changed considerably since 1939, largely because of the powerful argument of Mises' *Human Action*. We stand by our original theoretical analysis, however. For instance, the statement that "every entrepreneur confronted with a downward-sloping long-run demand schedule is a monopolist . . . ." holds because of the crucial words "long run." But today the author is inclined to regard even the largest "price searchers," apart from local public utilities, as having very little exploitative power;[12] although when corporations *which collude* are large, the dangers of abuse are magnified. And it must be admitted that, when the private use of coercive power is acquiesced in, the possibilities of exploitation are undeniable.

17, 18, 19

---

[11] W. H. HUTT, *Politically Impossible . . .?*
[12] See pp. 221–22.

But in practice antitrust (or similar) government action tends nearly always to protect high-cost competitors or politically powerful competitors rather than protect the *competitive process.* Hence we judge that, unless there is clear evidence of collusion, nonintervention should be presumed to be more likely to result in the elimination of enforced idleness or withheld capacity than intervention. Moreover, when interindustry competition is brought into the reckoning, the case for tolerance of large corporations (incapable of collusion within themselves) is increased. We do not suggest that the *presumption* of the beneficence of largeness of scale of operations can never be upset. But there is a case for antitrust-type intervention if the controlling authority is explicitly instructed that neither corporation size nor high profits shall be regarded as, in themselves, proofs of monopolistic abuse; and that only *concrete evidence* of (i) a plan to exclude or (ii) the actual exclusion of men or assets from any area, industry, occupation or firm[13] shall be regarded as justification for antitrust proceedings.

---

[13] Or concrete evidence of a plan to shut in, or of the actual shutting in of men or assets into any area, industry, occupation or firm.

Chapter XI

Strike Idleness and Aggressive Idleness

1

The distribution of monopoly gains among
cooperant monopolists is indeterminate, and may
depend upon "reasonableness"

In discussing the relations between cooperant stages of production in the last chapter, we ignored an important consideration which may arise when two or more of these stages are monopolized. Idleness of a different kind may result from the arrangement of distribution among the owners of *cooperant* sets of productive operations (e.g., firms, and groups of workers) who are sharing in the benefits of restrictionism. It has its origin in distributive considerations but is otherwise completely different from that which is the product of bargaining among the owners of *competing* resources. When purely cooperant activities are concerned, no question of quotas arises. But the proportion of the monopoly gains which accrues to each cooperator is just as indeterminate as the size of quotas. The monopolists' optimum output (which is to their collective interest) is again independent of the shares of the monopoly revenue which each cooperant party happens to get. If output falls short of the optimum at any time, then arrangements are conceivable under which no cooperant monopolist will lose while the whole will gain. As no principle of distribution exists, however, it is once again probable, as we have already pointed out, that "reasonableness" will dictate the solution. And "reasonableness" usually means in practice a division of the spoils not diverging greatly from the proportions in which aggregate revenues have been shared in the past. The result is expressed in the prices charged for monopolistically controlled cooperant services at each stage of the productive process. To some extent contracts may give permanence to any system of distribution which develops. But "vertical" monopolies which are not held together by complete amalgamation appear to rest in the long run upon little more than tacit understandings reinforced by custom and the acceptance of the *status quo*. It is not surprising, then, that each cooperant firm or group still wishes to get more for itself out of the benefits achieved by exploiting consumers.

2

The distribution of monopoly gains may depend upon bargaining, in which case "strike idleness" may arise

* But as there are no principles other than that which is based on the maintenance of existing rights, it is obvious that a deadlock must sometimes arise. A price is demanded which the next cooperant producer in the chain of production refuses to pay at all. His response is not to *cut down* his purchases but to *cease buying* altogether. Consequently, two sets of resources stand idle; and unless there are stocks of semifinished goods ahead, and unless previous cooperant producers can manufacture for stock, the whole chain of production will be brought to a standstill. This will be the result if interlopers (i.e., "blacklegs") are not attracted in and substitutes are not available. We can call it "strike idleness" because the strike, organized by a trade union, is the most common case of the actual phenomenon. But the term "strike idleness" as we have used it, applies to all of the resources rendered idle, and not merely to those owned by the party which takes the initiative in demanding a price change in respect of productive services being bought or sold. It is futile to try to distinguish "the aggressor" from "the defender," unless we call the party which demands a *change,* "the aggressor." The strike and the lockout are of identical nature. Thus, in the labor contract issue, in both cases the workers collectively demand a previously existing or a new wage-rate (or conditions similarly affecting costs) and refuse to supply any labor at all unless it is conceded; and in both cases "the employer" (or "employers" collectively) refuses to engage any labor at all at the wage-rate insisted upon.

3

When competing firms operate over
more than one set of cooperant productive processes,
distribution may be arranged through "demarcations,"
which may be enforced by strikes

We must now consider the fact that "withheld capacity" arrangements among a number of *competing* firms, each of which operates over *several stages* of the productive process, may take a different form. Agreements may be expressed, not in quotas, but in "demarcations." Each firm will consent to specialize for the future on, say, a particular process and give up the others. Especially where this policy has been followed, but in many other conceivable circumstances, the resulting *firms* may stand in both an *actually* cooperant and a *potentially competing* relationship to one another. And even where a cooperant firm or group cannot *itself* compete by invading other stages of production, it may frequently be in a position to supply interlopers in a subsequent process. Hence it may indirectly be in a potentially competing position. We frequently find a like situation in the *internal* relations of organized labor. The essence of the quarrel between "craft" and "industrial" unionism arises out of circumstances of this kind. In respect of the claims of cooperant groups, however, it is seldom a collusive *agreement* that binds the monopoly together; it is tradition and the recognition of a vested interest which determines each group's functions (and indirectly their claims) under a demarcation scheme. In all of these circumstances, because of this twofold—cooperant and competing—relationship, the strike may be used against potentially *competing* firms or groups. When employed in this way, the "strike" has much the same significance as "aggressive selling." It may be used to enforce "joint monopoly," that is, to prevent cooperant monopolists from invading spheres tacitly or formally forbidden to them, or to prevent them from dealing with outside interlopers who may wish to operate in some other stage of the productive process. This is manifested in the relations of organized labor to "the employers," i.e., the shareholders. The strike is used to prevent "the employers" from dealing with interloping labor. And all coercive enforcement of "demarcations" is of the same nature.

4
"Strike idleness" does not arise from
"withheld capacity" unless a cooperant producer resists
in order to force a sharing of the monopoly gains

It is important that the "strike" should not be confused

with "withheld capacity." Let us suppose that in a field of production in which competitive institutions are freely functioning at the outset, the workers succeed in combining and suddenly demand together an increased wage-rate. If the capitalists *really* stand in a competing relationship with one another, the effect will be, as in any other increase of costs, that output will fall and the burden will be partly transferred (through a price increase) to consumers. The transfer may be either direct, or through the next stage of production. So far, there will have been "withheld capacity" on the part of labor. Suppose that there are no substitutes for the labor and no further labor-saving organization is possible; and suppose the resulting commodity price to bring the maximum aggregate receipts from the sale of the final product. The monopoly-revenue part of these receipts is available for sharing among *all* the parties to production. Hence, if the "capitalists" understand the position, and wish to preserve their former income, they *can* share in the spoils. They can do this by coming to a collective decision concerning the wage-rate which they will pay. *There is no strike* unless there is action based on such a decision (or unless the capitalists resist with altruistic intentions, being unwilling to see consumers exploited). Until the capitalists acting in collusion—or in the case of single capitalists possessing some monopoly advantage, acting singly—refuse to give employment except on terms agreed among themselves, the idleness caused is merely "withheld capacity" on the part of the workers. The essence of the strike is that it is temporary, and in intention coercive. The coercion is based on the power to dislocate the process of "roundabout" production by the withdrawal of temporarily or permanently, imperfectly or absolutely, irreplaceable resources. In a "pure" strike between two parties, each side believes that the other will be the more burdened or inconvenienced, and counts on the other side's continued waste of its services forcing it to acquiesce. And the position can be equally simply conceived of when several cooperant parties are involved. But in practice the position is not so simple. It is complicated because potential interlopers usually stand ominously near, and because cooperant monopolists are tacitly threatening to bring in such interlopers, if unreasonableness is persisted in; and because the coercion of the strike is used for other purposes than fighting over the distribution of the value of the product of a set of operations under conditions of monopoly. These problems do not now concern us, however. Our present object is to distinguish clearly between idleness of "withheld capacity" and "strike idleness."

5

"Aggressive idleness" arises from the
maintenance of unutilized capacity with a view to
aggressive selling against potential interlopers

*   There is yet another reason why producers in a trade may desire the preservation of equipment in idleness. They may desire it collectively rather than individually, as a means of aggression against interlopers (the case of "aggressive idleness"). Far from being a disadvantage in these circumstances, the idle equipment must be thought of as a protection for the monopolists collectively, worth much more to them than its scrap value; for it confers the power to sell aggressively in order to crush *new interlopers*. Hence it stands as a constant menace to would-be interlopers. Restriction schemes are threatened less from *internal quarrels* than from the danger of competition from outside. It is probably *interlopers* rather than those who are already sharing in the spoils who most often cause the disintegration of collusive monopolies. Indeed, it seems probable that the greater part of that divergence of interest within, expressed chiefly through quota-hunting, would cease entirely if the permanence of a cartel could be assured by the suppression of all external competition. There is every motive therefore for keeping idle capacity in existence for the specific purpose of deterring interlopers. The motive may usually be but vaguely present in the minds of cartel authorities. But they are conscious of the power which it confers, even if hardly aware of its origin. We may call such idle capacity "aggressive idleness."[1] It is relevant internally as well as externally because every member of a cartel, for instance, is a potential interloper. He actually becomes an interloper the moment he breaks the understanding or collective agreement by cutting price or exceeding his quota. The idle equipment may be aggressively employed (through discrimination or otherwise) on rare occasions only; but its aggressive function is fulfilled by the threat implied in its mere presence. When it is *engaged* in an act of aggression, it is, curiously enough, no longer idle. The distinction between "participating" and "aggressive" idleness is not always clear when internal relations are considered, although in principle the distinction is plain enough. Capacity provided with aggressive intent may lead to participating rights being conferred. If the maintenance of the capacity is then necessary for the continuance of these rights, it is in "participating idleness." If that necessity is due to the requirement of a continuous threat to internal price cutters,

---

[1] See HUTT, "Nature of Aggressive Selling," *Economica*, August 1935.

it is *also* aggressive. But rights acquired by internal aggression *need* not demand a permanent defense. Income rights so achieved come to be regarded as "reasonable," whatever their origin.[2]

---

[2] We can think of no parallel to "aggressive idleness" in the case of labor, although privileged labor groups may benefit from the condition in co-operant equipment.

Appendix

Notes and Comments on Chapter XI

Our assumption in paragraph 2 that "it is futile to try to distinguish 'the aggressor' from 'the defender' " and that "the strike and the lockout are of an identical nature" misses, we now believe, a vital distinction. Which party, workers or investors, assumes the risks of the agreement by accepting the residual claim on the value of the output? It is that party, labor or the supplier of the assets, which is committed to accepting contractual remuneration from the other party which can be said to have brought about a work stoppage, whatever terms it refuses, however "unreasonable" those terms are judged to be. There is no obstacle in the legal institutions of Western society to prevent a group of organized workers from agreeing to accept the residue and pay contractual remuneration in the form of rent or hire for the use of the fixed assets and interest on the loans with which they finance the acquisition of other inputs (including the group's own labor). Workers' remuneration would then be wages *plus* profits or *minus* losses, just as today the owners of assets are mostly remunerated by

2

interest *plus* profits or *minus* losses. The author has discussed the possibilities of such arrangements elsewhere.[1] Our present point is that, while the strike is clearly a coercive act, an entrepreneurial offer can never be rationally regarded as coercive, although an entrepreneur's shutting off of the workers' access to other employment offers or outlets would be.

5   We have not changed the term "aggressive selling" in paragraph 5 although the more appropriate and now accepted term for the practice is "predatory selling." In our present judgment the importance of "aggressive idleness" in assets is much less important than we believed it might be in 1939. Nevertheless, we have felt it necessary to refer to the condition because some economists regard it as quite important. My 1935 essay on the subject (in *Economica*) has been reprinted in the symposium, *Individual Freedom,* edited by Svetozar Pejovich and David Klingaman, Greenwood Press, Westport, Ct., 1975.

---

[1] HUTT, *Strike-Threat,* Chap. 6, entitled "The Employer Stereotype."

Chapter XII

Conclusion

1
This essay has concentrated on "idleness" issues and ignored "demand" issues

We have now dealt with all the "causes" of idleness.   *
Yet the subject matter of this essay differs fundamentally from that of most recent discussions of "unemployment." This is because we have rigidly separated "idleness" issues from what are usually regarded as "demand" issues. Our approach has meant that the principal topics of contemporary theorizing, namely, certain forces behind the movement of demand schedules for the services of different sets of resources, have been deliberately ignored. We have said nothing about the sort of things commonly discussed in connection with variations of "demand in general." We are, however, justified in claiming that we have dealt with the "causes" of idleness. For whatever the demand schedule for the services of particular resources may be, if those resources are idle, then one or more of the causes appropriate to the different types of idleness that we have distinguished must be present. The movement of individual demand schedules is certainly relevant because the *extent* of the

various kinds of idleness in the particular resources concerned will *frequently* tend in practice to vary inversely with
such movements. But in respect of each type of idleness,
considered in isolation, the removal of the one specific
cause will lead to the complete cessation of the unemployment of the type in question, irrespective of the state of the
demand schedule. This does not mean that an attempt to
consider each type of idleness, in each case, in isolation,
could lead to a realistic or useful view of the employment
question; for different conditions of idleness in one line of
production may obviously react upon those in others. The
definitions we have introduced enable us to conceive of
proximate causes only. But such causes are important and
there is an indefensible tendency to ignore them in contemporary discussions. We may say that forces expressed
through the relevant demand schedules in particular sets
of productive operations sometimes control the *potency* of
the different causes; but in each case, apart from that
of "valueless resources," the idleness ceases with the elimination of *a cause which is independent of those forces.*

2

The present analysis has introduced distinctions which are essential for any satisfactory study of the effects of demand variations

The peculiar scope which we have chosen may leave the
impression that the most important aspects of idleness have
in fact been overlooked. But the analysis here attempted
seems to be absolutely essential if satisfactory studies of the
effects of phenomena usually described as variations of "demand in general" or "general purchasing power" are to be
made. If the chaotic controversies in which this study at
present abounds are to be cleared up, the implications of

the different types of idleness which we have pointed out may have to be faced. We are not sure of the manner in which an application of our distinctions would modify recent inquiries into the nature of general purchasing power. But that they have a most important relevance is surely obvious. Take, for instance, the conceptions of "glut" and "gluttability." Does the existence of a glut of a commodity mean that all or some of the resources producing it are "valueless," or that in the glut situation it pays to "withhold capacity"? Surely the whole problem takes on a completely different complexion according to which interpretation is appropriate.

3
The application of the conceptions of this
essay to monetary theory has yet to be done

It has been alleged of more than one contribution to the social sciences that the author has left the impression of packing a trunk in preparation for a long voyage of exploration but has got no farther than his own doorstep. It may well be that others may set out on the travels for which we have here made preparations. We are not sure of what will be discovered, but a clear and simple map is urgently needed. At present, either the thinking behind or else the exposition of time-preference and liquidity-preference studies is hopelessly confused.

4
The conceptions of this essay
are relevant to the nonmonetary aspects of idleness

But this essay is intended to be much more than mere   *
trunk packing. We believe that the conceptions which it isolates are directly relevant to contemporary policy outside

the monetary field as well as to prospecting within it. Although currency controversies await solution, many of the most acute problems which confront the policymakers of today will survive any advance in scientific insight into currency theory, or growth of enlightenment in currency policy. May it not be that Marshall was shrewdly correct in his continuous preaching that the "only thing to be said about currency is that it is not nearly as important as it looks"? As the present writer emphasized some years ago, "it is easy to expect too much to be accomplished by an ideal monetary mechanism. The recognition of certain deficiencies in an existing regime may lead us to suppose that the right system of money, if we could only find it, would automatically correct the results of the refusal to make otherwise desirable adjustments in many spheres."[1] But "the perfect monetary system would not prevent the perpetual fight between productive efficiency (enforced where competition is effective), on the one hand, and the vested interests which determine the division of the value of productivity (as they can do when competition can be restricted), on the other hand."[2]

5
The conceptions of this essay are relevant to the trade cycle

The notion of variations in "prosperity" can be realistically studied in terms which assume the existence of the ideal monetary system. For is not "prosperity" in fact a distributive rather than a productive concept? Is not a policy which brings "prosperity" in its popular sense one

---

[1] *South African Journal of Economics*, December 1934, p. 476.
[2] Ibid., p. 477.

which protects or enhances rates of wages and rates of dividends? And are not these rates of return maintained or raised through the diversion of resources, some of which find inferior employments, and some of which remain in idleness? Does not the distribution of wage-earners tend to be more biased toward the less well-paid types of employment the higher the rates of payment that are insisted upon? And is it not obviously true that typical methods of dividend protection mean that new capital developments are prevented from taking place when they would supply productive services which the market indicates are most wanted —because the competitive effect of such development is felt to be too serious? Is that not at least a partial explanation of the popularity of schemes for subsidized public works in depression? Would we not be still likely to have, even under an ideal monetary system, the occasional emergence (often regarded as a cyclical emergence) of situations in which the apparent reasonableness on profitableness of the monopolistic withholding of productive capacity in the interests of dividends or wage-rates is increased? Would an ideal monetary system in fact put an end to the powerful and painful equalitarian tendencies which all the current attempts to restrict competition have been unable completely to suppress?

6
The conceptions of this essay may suggest the correct approach to the monetary aspects of idleness

Even before the days when the general form of classical monetary theory began to crystallize, it had been realized that the "quantity of money" was somehow a fundamental force in the determination of "prosperity." Mercantilist speculations reflected the conviction that scarcity of money was a major disadvantage to be overcome by State policy. And the refinements brought about during the foundation of orthodoxy in the late eighteenth century never denied the phenomena from which mercantilist beliefs had been derived. Hume observed that the entry of new money into the economic system had the effect of "exciting industry." And a large part of subsequent study has been indirectly devoted to discovering the exact genesis of such "excitement" of production. In this connection two suggestions appear to be implied by the argument of the thesis here presented: (i), that inquiries in this field ought to be directed in their first stages to the problem of whether the "excitement" brings value to valueless resources; or whether the repercussions of the "excitement" are primarily expressed in the dissolution of withheld capacity and enforced idleness, and only secondarily, if at all,[3] in enlarging the range of valuable resources; (ii), that inquiries in this field should examine the contention that both in the practical selection of monetary policies under political systems dominated by "pressure groups," and in the less tangible psychological influences determining typical preference for or tolerance of inflationary theories, the distributive effects have subconsciously loomed more important than the productive. We have suggested that the "prosperity" envisaged in monetary discussions has, in spite of the implication that the condition is accompanied by the absence of idleness, been more of a distributive than a productive concept. And although it is true that the cyclical idleness of resources

---

[3] The release of productive power may cause the range of valuable resources to *contract* rather than expand. See Chap. II, paras. 2 and 10.

seems to be a phenomenon of production and not of distribution, it has never been shown that there is anything more than a random periodicity in such cycles of idleness. Our present hypothesis concerning their "occasional emergence" certainly fits the facts as well as most other theories.

7
Wasteful idleness arises through the restriction of competition

Regrettable idleness, like other forms of "waste," seems to be the product of arrangements which allow private interest to triumph over social interest. It arises, in other words, because our laws permit competition to be restricted. Hence, no improvement of the monetary system alone is capable of eliminating causes of idleness while other existing institutions remain. And this essay has incidentally drawn attention to some of the defects in these institutions. For reform, we shall probably have to wait for the embodiment of social ideals in a *consistent* philosophy of the functions of the State and the convincing exposition of that philosophy.

Appendix

Notes and Comments on Chapter XII

In this chapter we discuss the relevance of our analysis of "idleness issues" to "demand issues," which we *say* we have "rigidly separated." Actually, the "demand issue" has come up several times, and it has been given further attention in the various chapter appendices.

In paragraph 4 we refer to an article we published two years before the appearance of Keynes' *General Theory*.[1] In that article we asserted that "the right system of money, if we could only find it, . . . would not prevent the perpetual fight between productive efficiency (enforced where competition is effective), on the one hand, and the vested interests which determine the division of the value of productivity (as they can when competition can be restricted), on the other hand." This is one of our conclusions to which Lindley Fraser objected in his 1939 review. He referred to the last paragraph in the book, in which it is explicitly concluded

---

[1] It was a review article (unsigned) of Lionel Robbins' *The Great Depression*. (*South African Journal of Economics*, December 1934.)

that "regrettable idleness . . . arises because our laws permit competition to be restricted." But if the definition of competition we have given on p. 154 is accepted, Fraser's objection can hardly be sustained.

7   On pp. 125 ff. we quoted and defended the assertion: "People are always unemployed by choice." Heyne and Johnson, whose phrase that is, do not imply that the other causes of idleness among former or potential workers that we have here classified and defined are unimportant. What the phrase *does* mean is that it is an "unemployed" person's reaction to all the other "causes" of unemployment of labor we have noticed which ultimately induces him to turn down immediately available employment possibilities. But what is officially *classed* as "unemployment" in this case may, as we have seen, be "job-search"—prospecting for the best employment outlets; and this is a most important form of *productive employment* under our definitions. And any rational policy aimed at dissolving wasteful idleness in labor must recognize courageously that this crucial form of productive activity is deplorably handicapped today by strike-threat enforcement of "the rate for the job."

We should remind the reader that the economists we quoted in Chapter V on "preferred idleness" all make it clear that they do not regard the choice of leisure as, in itself, blameworthy. We ourselves shared that judgment in 1939 (see p. 117), and provided that leisure is purchased, we still do. After all, he who expresses an increased preference for *unsubsidized leisure* pays for it. He does so by removing his bidding for nonmoney, to the material advantage of those whose demand for leisure does not change.

There is, however, what we believe to be a neglected

aspect of "preferred idleness." Leisure is a form of consumption[2] and as such acts as a *depressant* of the economy (just as production to replace the value of consumption, or to add to the stock of assets, acts as a *stimulant*). It follows that, in times of widespread unemployment, while no one would ordinarily want to discourage the consumption of leisure, one could well, in those circumstances, expect sophisticated humanitarians to try to persuade all employed workers to consent to longer hours of labor, without increased remuneration, in order, *for purely altruistic reasons,* to raise prospective yields to investment in noncompeting labor inputs for the replacement and growth of productive power. That would be the most effective way of raising the purchasing power of employment outlets generally.

For identical reasons, sophisticated humanitarians could well call upon governments not only to require organized labor to abandon feather-bedding and other so-called "make-work" devices, but to plead with industrialists to resort to labor-economizing machinery and managerial ingenuities, including automation, while at the same time removing obstacles, like the rate for the job (imposed by strike-threats or strikes), which restrain workers released by the economies achieved from actually making additional contributions to the source of demands. This they can do only by pricing their potential inputs for actual absorption into the real wages-flow as well as for absorption into an increased income flow from investment in additional assets.

The most appropriate initial step toward raising the

---

[2] *Ceteris paribus* the value of a person as "human capital" will decline when he reduces the value of his inputs into the common pool of production. All exterminations of value, whether purposeful or passive, are to be classed as "consumption."

probability that workers at present in "preferred idleness" could be induced to contribute to demand for services of labor generally, would be legislation to guarantee every worker, whether initially in sub-optimal employment or un-employed, the right of effective access to any bargaining table. This implies that he must have the basic right to accept any offer of employment at any wage contract, conditions of work or prospects which he believes to be more favorable than any alternative he thinks he will be able to discover. Such a reform[3] would, we predict, bring about so formidable an increase in the wages-flow and in income equality that, after a decade of experience of such a regime, the general abolition of the right to use coercive power privately in the labor market would become politically acceptable. An unparalleled gain in affluence and freedom would then have been won, and the long battle against unemployment and poverty would come to an end.

"One man's work is another man's employment," said Dean Josiah Tucker in the middle of the eighteenth century. The implications of this simple truth were latent in the theory of the division of labor as it developed from Mandeville to Adam Smith. And the vital principle itself was enunciated with remarkable clarity by James Mill and J. B. Say in the early years of the nineteenth century.

But economists nurtured in the Keynesian notion that consumption is *the source of* power to demand instead of the *extermination of* that power (and this means the majority of today's economists) have, even when they have at last recognized the validity of Say's law, failed to com-

---

[3] In the United States such a reform would mean the federal application of the rule of Clause 14b of the Taft-Hartley Act.

municate its significance to legislators and government executives.

During the 1976 presidential election in the United States, although unemployment and recession were major issues, we heard both candidates promising, without knowing that this was what they were in fact promising, to reduce the purchasing power of employment outlets by using taxed income to provide *boondoggling jobs*. By "boondoggling jobs" we mean remunerated activities which do not add to the uninflated value of aggregate real income.[4]

When governments promise to "create jobs," in that way they are indeed unwittingly committing themselves to destroy "job opportunities." If governments honestly wish to reduce unemployment, all they can do is to encourage or assist the pricing of labor's inputs consistently with market-clearing of the outputs into which those inputs are embodied. And the purpose of the required wage-rate adjustments is not *primarily* to secure employment for labor which is initially overpriced (given the justified entrepreneurial pessimism which reigns in recession), but to contribute to demands for labor in noncompeting productive activities generally.

There can never be *assured* employment in any particular occupation or industry as long as potential employees are— whether through collusion, private coercion, or government coercion on behalf of private privileged interests—denied the right to ask or accept whatever prices or conditions for the sale of their personal services (or the services of their

---

[4] "Real income," we should remind the reader, means the aggregate flow of "purchasing power" (as distinct from the aggregate flow of "money-spending power").

assets) that they judge will serve them best. Prices which do not exceed market-clearing values can alone ensure that *potential* contributions to output will become *realized* contributions. Yet subsequent to Keynes, almost a whole generation of economists has been brainwashed into believing that a properly designed and administered monetary or fiscal policy can assure "full employment," *irrespective of of how the pricing system is managed.*

Of course unanticipated inflation can crudely, unjustly, and temporarily improve coordination in the pricing system.[5] But if the rising price index causes renewed recourse to strike-threat pressures to restore real wage-rates in protected occupations, what has become known as "wage push" must cause the inflationary burden to become progressively and discernibly purposeless.

---

[5] "Unjustly" because those producers who have not been pricing their services or those of their assets above market-clearing values are penalized, at least initially, as well as those who had been responsible for such prices.

Addendum

The Concept of
Idle Money

1
What is "money"?

An important omission in the 1939 edition was any classi-
fication of money under the definitions presented. This
is a difficult topic with which to deal partly because it pre-
supposes a clear notion of exactly what "money" is. However, the definition of money that we are about to submit is
likely to be dismissed at first by many economists who
believe (as does the present author himself) that a return to
the pre-1914 type of gold standard (at whatever parity is
judged most likely to bring about stability of average prices)
could win great benefits for mankind.[1] Yet many enthusiasts
for the restoration of such a standard hold that it is important
to distinguish "money" (in the sense of a commodity) from

---

[1] Our own position in respect of gold as a monetary standard is discussed
in our *Say's Law,* pp. 128–32. Very briefly, the most that can be hoped for
from a readoption of a currency convertible at a carefully judged value of
gold, would be not perfect monetary stability, but something incomparably
better than the monetary chaos and the consequent general economic chaos
which has ruled since 1931.

"credit" (in the sense of checking account deposits or notes), even if the "credit" is effectively convertible into the chosen commodity on demand. Thus, a recent contributor has declared categorically, "gold is money." And several economists of stature still insist upon a definition which distinguishes between "money" and "credit." They usually envisage "money" as gold (or as some other commodity, or as a document wholly backed by a defined and concrete bundle of commodities, such as was advocated by Frank D. Graham and Benjamin Graham), and they tacitly envisage "credit" as all other money under the definition below. But economists who think this distinction is useful ought to perceive that, whatever kind of gold money (or gold standard) they regard as ideal, whether under the fractional reserve system or otherwise, the following definition will cover it. By "money" we mean:

> All assets the value of which arises, or is enhanced, because they are demanded and held *wholly or partially* for the monetary services they render, i.e., for the express purpose of exchange for nonmoney goods or services in the future. This definition covers currency in circulation, demand deposits, *and* (here my usage differs from what is conventional)[2] the pure money equivalent of "near-money" or "money substitutes"—"hybrid assets" which are partly nonmoney but which provide monetary services and are therefore partly money also.[3]

---

[2] In the quantity theory identity ($MV \equiv PT$) as we use it (purely for exposition purposes), M includes the pure money equivalent of "near-money." As other economists use the identity, the effects of "near-money" are represented (most misleadingly in our judgment) under V. (See pp. 261–62.)

[3] On the notion of the "pure money equivalent" of such "hybrid" assets, see HUTT, *Keynesianism,* p. 92.

2
The types of "idleness" we have analyzed
for nonmoney can never be discerned in money,
except for pseudo-idleness

We can now consider the crucial question: How relevant to the condition which is commonly described as "idle money" or "idle money balances" are the various notions which we have here distinguished for idleness in nonmoney? We propose to show that virtually nothing resembling *withheld capacity* or *enforced idleness* (and hence nothing resembling *participating idleness*) can be found in money. Nor can we conceive of money as such ever becoming *valueless,* although when the money *unit* loses value in a runaway inflation, the value of the unit may eventually become infinitely small. But as that happens new forms of money will almost certainly be superseding it. What had previously been nonmoney assets will have their value enhanced because they are demanded not only for the normal services they render but for monetary purposes. Cigarettes are the stock example. Such assets are of the "hybrid" type. Apparent idleness in money is, we shall see, pseudo-idleness.

3
The yield to money held

Money, in whatever form, is invested in because it is productive, either (a) in the sense that "capital consumer goods" in households are productive, rendering income in the form of "gratifications" (e.g., as with a diamond, or an antique, or a valuable picture); (b) in the sense that, as capital, inventories of economically perishable goods (goods of relatively short prospectively profitable life span) are productive; or (c) in the sense that many nonmoney "producer goods" are passively productive (e.g., the site of a factory or shop, the building itself, or its fixtures and equipment). Such assets are physically "idle," but not necessarily in the sense of being unemployed. And one invests in money (i) in one's wallet and personal checking account, up to the point at which the prospective marginal yield in terms of "gratifications" (mainly convenience) has fallen to the rate of interest,[4] or (ii) in the cash registers and checking account of a business, up to the point at which the prospective marginal yield from investment in it—a pecuniary return—has fallen to the rate of interest. Money differs from other assets in this respect only because it is completely nonspecific. Thus, if through unwise or unlucky forecasts one *overinvests* in particular nonmoney assets or assets mixes, one may suffer a considerable loss, in spite of possible disinvestment of the excess, whereas in the case of money, redundant stocks can always be disinvested, without further delay and loss, as soon as the redundancy is perceived.

4

Speculatively held money is productive, not idle

Investment in or disinvestment from money may take place for speculative motives. In this respect again, money

---

[4] This is the position in respect of *all* "consumers' capital goods." For instance, if I possess a Rembrandt which I could sell for a million dollars, it is obvious that I value the aggregate flow of gratifications I enjoy from its possession at not less than the current rate of interest on a million dollars; and when I decide how much to invest altogether in works of art for my personal pride and pleasure (and that of my family and visitors to my home), there must be a point at which I shall value further increments of

resembles nonmoney assets. If it is believed that the real value of the money unit is likely to fall, or that the market rate of interest is likely to fall, people will economize in liquidity and hold smaller money balances. Nonmoney will rise in profitability in relation to money. And when the real value of the money unit is believed to be rising, people will sacrifice the prospective yields from some nonmoney in order to increase their money balances. In the former case, the prospective relative productivity of money declines; and in the latter case, the prospective relative productivity of money rises. We cannot, therefore, usefully describe *abnormally* large money balances as *"idle* money," for money is then judged to be abnormally productive.[5]

5
What has been termed
"idle money" is really in "pseudo-idleness"

Money as such is always passively rendering the service of availability, which is the most important form of the productive condition we call *"pseudo-*idleness." In this respect, money held for business purposes resembles closely the inventories (materials, work in progress and finished products) which are in process of continuous realization and replenishment. Just as the purchasing budget of a firm normally plans for the replacement of sales over the budgetary period, so does its finance budget plan for the replacement of its stock of money, a stock the prospective return to which (as with other inventories) may be subject to sea-

---

capital devoted to the acquisition of works of art at less than I value the additional utility attainable therefrom.

[5] Of course the forecasts on which judgments of profitability depend may happen to be wrong, as with all assets and assets mixes.

sonal and other changes. And exactly the same is true of
the economy of the household. Inventories of money (in
wallets or checking accounts) have to be replenished for
exactly the same reason that inventories of food in pantries
and refrigerators, inventories of soap, detergents and household gadgets subject to depreciation, and inventories of
clothing (being gradually worn out or consumed through
fashion-change obsolescence) have to be replaced.

6
Money does not render its services
by circulating but by being ready to circulate

The notion of *idle* money seems to have arisen out of the
age-old fallacy that money performs its services by circulating, whereas in reality its services, which are performed
simply by its being possessed and *ready for circulation,*
cease for the one holder the moment the ownership is transferred to another because the purpose of having invested in
it has ceased for the transferor and is about to begin for the
transferee. For centuries money has been aptly described
as "lubricating" the process of commerce, meaning that it
has been economizing the process of discovering and com-
municating knowledge necessary for the fruitful exchange
of the products of men and assets. But this does not upset
the principle that *money performs its function just by being
held.* It simply illustrates the origins of nonspeculative
demand for money.

7
A money unit conforms to the ordinary laws of value

It may be objected that it is possible to reduce the number
of money units, thus making each unit more scarce and

valuable, which is an exact parallel to raising the value of other commodities by the contrived scarcity of withheld or diverted capacity! The answer is that the money unit certainly conforms to the ordinary laws of value, just like all other assets, and that if demand for the services of money increases (i.e., if its prospective productivity rises relative to nonmoney, while "money supply," in the sense of the number of money units, remains constant), the value of the money *unit* will rise. But this rise in value is a natural scarcity value and not a contrived scarcity value, however unwise deflation may be at any time. When some persons or firms decide to hold more money units, leaving fewer for others, they are not *withholding* the money they acquire or retain. They are investing in it. They are bidding quite freely against others for the money they hold, add to or discard. About the year 1924, we heard a prominent industrialist in Britain, who was attacking the British banks for supporting the return to gold and the deflation which it implied, say: "If I were a steel producer I should naturally support any policy which increased the value of steel. The banks, being money producers, may be expected to support a policy which is intended to increase the value of the pound." But we cannot rightly describe any deflationary action, required by the contractural obligations to which a monetary authority may be bound, as the contrivance of monetary scarcity. Nor can central banks *plus* other banks and financial institutions produce or consume money in the sense of the *aggregate purchasing power* of money stocks. What they *can* do is to determine the number of containers of that purchasing power. That is, they *can* determine *aggregate money-spending power.*

8
Determinants of the "money supply"

Let us consider just how the banking system as a whole determines the number of money units. Whenever the money unit has some *constant* defined value,[6] a contract exists under which those institutions through which lending and borrowing are primarily facilitated, i.e., through which credit is issued or withdrawn, are committed so to control the process that the aggregate value of money measured in terms of *actual* money units (conventionally represented by the symbol M) is caused to vary more or less in proportion to the aggregate *real* value of money assets, which is the same aggregate magnitude but measured in abstractly conceived money units of constant purchasing power (which, in some of our other writings, we have represented by the symbol M_r).[7] If the unit has no *defined* value, its purchasing power must depend upon arbitrary political decisions; but because *some* stability of real value is usually expedient, it is still normally essential that (especially when the expectations of the people are a powerful factor) M should not be caused or allowed to increase too rapidly in proportion to M_r. *Deliberate* deflations—such as that through which Britain returned to the gold standard in the 1920s and then half-heartily attempted to persevere with—seem always to have been the fulfillment of a contract.[8]

---

[6] We say *constant* defined value because a defined value *could* be a depreciating value. Thus, some economists have advocated a steady fall in the real value of the money unit.

[7] In practice, monetary standards (e.g., the gold standard) have been chosen or persevered with because society has believed that these standards have *inter alia* guaranteed a sufficiently stable real value of the money unit.

[8] The world had accepted in good faith the British promise (during World

9
Determinants of the aggregate real value of money

The value M_r is determined, on the demand side, solely
by the prospective productiveness of money, expressed as
the demand for money; and on the other (the supply) side
by all the factors which determine the prospective profitableness of lending (not only on the part of banks but of
all lenders), namely, the extent to which the magnitude
and composition of the assets stock provide (a) goods with
the attributes of moneyness, (b) appropriate collateral or
cover for loans, and (c) the extent to which, for other reasons, credit-worthiness can be offered by such owners of
assets as find it profitable to borrow. Using the conventional
quantity theory identity, $MV \equiv PT$,[9] the demand for monetary services will tend to vary with (i) T (aggregate output)
and (ii) $\frac{1}{V}$ (all factors other than output which influence
the demand for monetary services).

10
As with other assets, money may be wastefully used

Money can be acquired for use (i.e., held) only in competition with others who also want to hold it. Everyone can
hold as much as he judges to be profitable provided he
demands it by offering nonmoney at its market-clearing

War I) ultimately to redeem her currency in gold; the world had lent to her
cheaply in consequence; and the reduction of M relative to M_r was merely
the process of settling debt as distinct from default. Whether Britain had to
pay too big a price for collective morality is a question of some interest.

[9] As we use this identity, P is an appropriate price index, T is aggregate
output measured in "real" terms; while V, which has conventionally meant
"velocity"—the rate of turnover of money—is not used here in that sense
but as explained in the text.

value. But he cannot hold as much of it as he would like: he can only have as much as he judges it will be worth sacrificing nonmoney for. And if the defined value of the money unit is in terms of constant purchasing power, it simply means that the average nonmoney value he must sacrifice to get any additional money unit will also be constant. We maintain therefore that, in respect of money, there can be nothing resembling the withholding of capacity or its diversion into sub-optimal uses. There can, of course, be misjudgment about its productivity, so that it will be wastefully used, to its owner's (and society's) detriment. In this respect, it does not differ from nonmoney assets.

11
Banking institutions may exploit

Nothing we have said implies that the banking system may not be in a position to exploit the community in respect of charges for its essential services, especially when it is organized monopolistically through a central bank. But that is a separate point with which we are not here concerned.[10]

12
Unproductive investment in money is essentially wasteful use, not idleness

To sum up, the concept of "idle money" is and always has been inherently defective, just as has the related *pre-*

---

[10] A theoretical complication is the fact that among the assets which perform monetary services are some which perform other services also (see pp. 253–54). Those assets which, when held for monetary purposes in business, still offer a pecuniary yield below the long-term rate of interest, are commonly known as "near-money" or "money substitutes." Preferring to call them "hybrid money" or "hybrid assets," we have shown in another work that it is possible to determine their pure-money equivalent (*Keynesianism*, p. 92).

Keynesian concept of "hoarded money." The market-clearing prices of inventories of *non*money are not necessarily exceeded when increased inventories are built up by their owners. The inventories are investments in the production of "time utilities" and other nonmaterial services.[11] Similarly, the market-clearing value of money units is not exceeded when, because on balance people correctly perceive that monetary policy aims at deflation, they invest more in money inventories. Speculation in money must always assist, never frustrate correctly discerned intentions of central banks and treasuries. Speculators' profits in this case are, as in all instances of profits achieved in the absence of some contrived scarcity or contrived plenitude, rewards for productive services rendered. But investment in money may be due, on occasion, as we mentioned in paragraph 10, to entrepreneurial error. Then, just as in the case of wrong entrepreneurial decisions about the amount and composition of investment in nonmoney, the decision-maker will be penalized. But under the free market system, all such errors (equally in the nonmoney and the money spheres) are penalized more or less in proportion to the magnitude of the error. Similarly, wise or lucky entrepreneurial decisions will be rewarded in rough proportion to the wisdom or luck of the decision-maker.

---

[11] *Ceteris paribus,* the cheaper the costs of information and communication happen to be, the smaller will be the profitableness of investment in inventories of both money and nonmoney, i.e., the less productive will be the *pseudo*-idleness state.

Index

This book was linotype set in the Times Roman series of type. The face was designed to be used in the news columns of the *London Times*. The *Times* was seeking a type face that would be condensed enough to accommodate a substantial number of words per column without sacrificing readability and still have an attractive, contemporary appearance. This design was an immediate success. It is used in many periodicals throughout the world and is one of the most popular text faces presently in use for book work.

Book design by Design Center, Inc., Indianapolis
Typography by Typoservice Corporation, Indianapolis
Printed by Hilltop Press, Inc., Indianapolis